Moving Materials
Physical Delivery in Libraries

Edited by Valerie Horton and Bruce Smith

American Library Association

Chicago   2010

Valerie Horton became the first director of the Colorado Library Consortium, a statewide provider of courier service, continuing education, cooperative purchase, and other library support services, in November 2004. She was previously director of the Mesa State College library and head of systems at New Mexico State University. During her tenure in New Mexico, Valerie received an ALA International Fellowship and spent a year in the Republic of Trinidad and Tobago, where she consulted with the Office of the Prime Minister on automating the country's public, school, and government libraries. She started her professional career as a systems librarian at Brown University after graduating from the University of Hawaii in 1984.

Bruce Smith is the delivery services coordinator for the South Central (Wisconsin) Library System (SCLS), which provides service to its fifty-two member libraries in seven counties and also serves as the primary statewide library delivery service for the Wisconsin Libraries' Delivery Network. Previous to his fourteen years at SCLS, Bruce spent six years in the transportation business in the areas of building supply, grocery, and expedited package delivery.

The paper used in this publication meets the minimum requirements of American National Standard for Information Sciences—Permanence of Paper for Printed Library Materials, ANSI Z39.48-1992. ⊗

Library of Congress Cataloging-in-Publication Data
Moving materials : physical delivery in libraries / edited by Valerie Horton and Bruce Smith.
    p.   cm.
   Includes bibliographical references and index.
   ISBN 978-0-8389-1001-6 (alk. paper)
   1. Direct delivery of books—United States. 2. Library materials—Transportation—United States. 3. Interlibrary loans—United States. 4. Library cooperation—United States—Case studies.
   I. Horton, Valerie.   II. Smith, Bruce, 1967–
Z712.M68 2010
025.6—dc22   2009025124

ISBN-13: 978-0-8389-1001-6

Printed in the United States of America

14   13   12   11   10   5   4   3   2   1

Contents

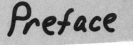

Preface

Our decision to write a book about library physical delivery developed out of the confluence of three factors. In Denver in September 2006 more than 125 people involved in library delivery from the United States and Canada met to share their successes and frustrations. This conference was the first time that any group had met solely to discuss physical delivery. Those who attended learned there was a wealth of information to be shared concerning the topic.

The second factor was our discovery that there is nearly no professional literature related to the field. On occasion a book or article on electronic delivery mentions physical delivery, but only in passing. The bibliography in this book contains several unpublished documents and press releases that make up the bulk of current physical delivery information in the professional literature.

The final factor was the staggering realization of the sheer number of items libraries are picking up, sorting, and delivering. Speaker after speaker at the 2006 conference spoke about the millions of items they were shipping each year. Large public libraries with numerous branches are moving ten, twelve, or even twenty million items a year. Many libraries are running out of funds for mailing interlibrary loan transactions because of the growth in requests. OCLC reports that it will pass ten million transactions a year, growing at a staggering rate of 100,000 transactions a year.

In Wisconsin, the delivery service Bruce Smith runs is shipping eleven million items annually. The wear and tear on his delivery equipment, personnel, and library materials is a constant problem. Smith's shop runs a fleet of twenty-four trucks that provide direct delivery to 194 libraries and 119 outreach locations, logging in 750,000 miles a year. With a staff of twenty-four full-time employees and twenty part-time drivers, Smith has firsthand experience in dealing with all the issues related to managing an in-house delivery system.

In 2004, Valerie Horton took over the management of the Colorado Library Courier, a delivery system that had been in place since the late 1980s. Horton's first year was spent consolidating the state's delivery under one pricing model and a single delivery vendor. Horton's second year was spent recovering from that vendor's going out of business. Colorado's library courier delivers five million items to four hundred libraries statewide.

In preparing for this book, we toured numerous delivery services, talked to dozens of people at conferences and by phone, and participated in a national survey (discussed elsewhere in this book). We have accumulated a substantial amount of experience in dealing with physical delivery operations, but to make sure the book's coverage is comprehensive and offers as many points of view as possible we have called on the expertise of nine other contributors. For their contributions, we thank Lori Ayre, Brenda Bailey-Hainer, Robin Dean, Ivan Gaetz, David Millikin, Jim Myers, Lisa Priebe, Greg Pronevitz, and Melissa Stockton. We also thank the three vendors who gave of their time to help us build an understanding of the logistics industry: Becky Atcheson (then of RR Donnelly Logistics), Ken Bartholomew (American Courier), and David Millikin (OCLC). We hope this book increases the dialogue and information available to managers who deal on a daily basis with the physical delivery of library materials.

Part One

The Current Landscape
of Physical Delivery

1

Delivery: The Forgotten Function

Valerie Horton

It is difficult to think of a topic in current librarianship that is deader than the mail delivery of library books. Few librarians have given this subject even a moment's thought. For many years, the literature on the subject has been nil.

Robert T. Jordan, 1970

What has changed in library delivery since Jordan's 1970 assessment? Quite a bit. Several public libraries have long-established home delivery service, and most deliver to the homebound. Colleges now routinely deliver library materials to distance education students. But how many librarians stop for even a moment before building a new branch to consider that home delivery costs about the same as running a medium-sized branch? In the coming chapters we explore the current state of library delivery, from home delivery through outsourcing with commercial carriers.

Public libraries had become common in larger cities by the late 1800s, with branch libraries opening early in the twentieth century. Borrowing between libraries started early as well, with the ALA first publishing the U.S. Interlibrary Loan Code in 1917 and adopting it in 1919. Throughout the twentieth century, resource sharing evolved and expanded to meet patron needs in a more cost-effective manner.

Resource sharing involves three elements: *discovery, request,* and *delivery.* Discovery is identifying where an item is located—usually through a citation from a print source, a standard interlibrary loan (ILL) transaction, a consortium's global catalog, or any number of Internet searches. Some states now offer statewide ILL systems, making it much easier to discover the contents of small library collections which in the past where not part of OCLC WorldCat or other union catalogs.

The second piece in the resource-sharing process is the request for the item. Again, in a standard ILL transaction using a service like OCLC or a statewide ILL system, the request function is part of the service's software design. With consortium borrowing, either the software has a custom borrowing module such as Innovative Interfaces' INN-Reach system or the consortium may turn on a hold function across all library collections in the global catalog. In either case, direct patron borrowing allows the patron rather than library staff to make the request for an item from another library.

The final piece of the transaction is the delivery. Traditionally, ILL has been through the U.S. Postal Service, but with the advent of consortium borrowing numerous library delivery services have developed across the country.

Despite this long history of resource sharing, the profession has spent little time studying, exploring, or writing about delivery, with the exception of electronic delivery. This lack of formal literature on physical delivery has required us to develop several categories of library delivery systems for use in this book. These categorizations are meant to provide a basis for analyzing the spectrum of delivery activities occurring in libraries and consortia today.

ORGANIZATIONAL MODELS OF DELIVERY

To understand library delivery, a manager needs to understand the organization and financing options available for various delivery methods and models. There are several ways of categorizing delivery services. One is to look at who is providing the actual delivery, such as the post office, overnight commercial carriers like FedEx, regional commercial carriers, or in-house fleets. Another is to organize the systems by which regions are served. In this scheme, delivery can be divided by city or county borders, regional areas within a state, state boundaries, multi-state systems, or national delivery.

The first and most traditional form of delivery between noninternal branch systems is the U.S. Postal Service (USPS). The USPS has long been used to ship library materials between unassociated libraries across the country and the world. In some states, the USPS is the only delivery method available for sharing items between libraries.

Internal branch delivery is long established and is probably the best known method of delivery by library patrons. In its most traditional application, internal branch delivery is used between public library branches or within a university system. Typically in this model the public library owns a fleet of in-house trucks or vans and pays drivers to run regular routes between the branch buildings. For colleges and universities, the library shares space on an existing delivery service run by the main institution.

As library consortia and regional library systems have grown and launched union catalogs, they have likewise created delivery systems to support resource sharing. These delivery services expanded to include libraries at considerable distances from the originating source and also different types of libraries. Regional delivery serving libraries within a relatively close proximity is common, such as deliveries to all the libraries in an urban and related suburban areas. But many delivery services have expanded to cover entire states and even to cross multiple state borders.

Commercial overnight carriers such as FedEx and UPS are used by many library systems and consortia to provide rapid delivery. Pennsylvania uses UPS to deliver half a million items statewide each year. Many academic consortia use overnight carriers because speed is important, particularly for medical and research-oriented institutions. Though commercial overnight carriers are expensive, the ability to track an item anywhere during the process and the guarantee of overnight delivery make them a popular option.

Most libraries use multiple delivery systems. For instance, a large academic library might use the USPS for out-of-state and international ILL, a regional courier for a local consortium, and an overnight commercial service to connect to other research institutions.

Delivery services often use multiple methods as well. For example, MINITEX delivers directly to libraries and regional delivery hubs in Minnesota and North and South Dakota. This region includes some libraries physically isolated from major population centers and freeways and with very low ILL borrowing rates. Direct delivery to these small libraries is not cost-effective, so MINITEX uses a combination of UPS and USPS for a small percentage of its overall delivery. MINITEX also links with the Wisconsin delivery service to share items, primarily OCLC ILL transactions across state borders.

One fact is clear: delivery decisions are always made on the basis of local conditions. For instance, having access to a garage and shipping space may well lead an organization to purchase a fleet of trucks; lack of that same garage space may lead an organization to an outsource solution. The delivery speed necessary to meet a researcher's demand drives delivery to an expensive but rapid overnight commercial carrier. The existence of several regional commercial carriers influenced Colorado's decision to use a vendor to provide statewide delivery; the absence of regional carriers despite similar terrain has made it difficult for Idaho to provide the same service. Local circumstances directly affect the nature of a library's delivery services.

INTERNALLY MANAGED DELIVERY VERSUS OUTSOURCED COMMERCIAL PROVIDERS

What conditions make building an in-house delivery system desirable? Managing a fleet of trucks and drivers requires the upfront capital to purchase equipment and the ability to manage complex personnel, routing, and equipment maintenance issues. The organization that chooses in-house delivery is making the commitment to run numerous routes typically five days a week in all types of weather and road conditions.

What makes a library system choose this option? Two main factors influence this decision. First, the expanded service often builds from a structure already in place to delivery within a large municipal branch system. This branch delivery infrastructure can easily be expanded to include nearby suburban libraries with minimal additional costs and problems. From there it can expand across larger regions or an entire state.

The second reason in-house managed delivery is chosen is that the delivery system has complete control over routes and the frequency and timing of internal deliveries. A large central library may need two or three deliveries a day to manage volume, and those items must arrive at specific times when staff are available. For many larger library systems in particular, which deal with millions of transactions, having internal control is crucial for efficient operations.

An alternative to in-house delivery is outsourcing to a commercial carrier. Knowledge of the logistics industry is needed to select a vendor and maintain a productive relationship. Employees of the carrier companies often have a different worldview and culture from that of library employees. So why do libraries choose outsourcing? Many organizations are either not equipped to manage an internal fleet or do not want the responsibility. Also, external vendor solutions can be cost-effective because the cost of library delivery may be shared, for example, with film, banking record, office supply, and pharmaceutical deliveries. The trade-off for shared delivery is less control of routes and delivery times.

The decision of which type of delivery to choose (USPS, commercial overnight service, in-house delivery, or outsourcing to regional carriers) is complex.

Many factors go into making the right choice. This book looks in depth at the pros and cons of each solution to guide the manager in making the choice that best fits their local circumstances.

GROWTH ISSUES AND TRENDS

Anyone who works with library delivery is pursuing two contradictory goals. One goal is to improve patron access to materials by making more and faster deliveries. But each delivery transaction has a cost and adds to wear and tear on library materials, so managers also want to reduce or eliminate deliveries. The manager is caught in a catch-22. The tension between these two conflicting goals, which can influence how delivery develops in a local system, is explored in the latter half of this book.

Libraries are using many interesting techniques to reduce deliveries. Floating collections have reduced delivery by nearly 70 percent in Hennepin County, Minnesota. In a floating collection, a library item does not have permanent shelf space at the originating building but remains at whatever library a patron returns it to. Floating collections are gaining popularity with public libraries, and recently academic libraries have started looking at incorporating the concept into their operations.

Another way of improving delivery efficiency is to reduce the time items stay in a hold queue. By delivering to the closest hold owner, rather than to the one first in line, the hold queue overall is reduced much faster than in the traditional first-in, first-out model. But this raises the question, is it ethical to bypass a patron first in line in a hold queue? Library managers are making decisions like this on a daily basis.

Another way of minimizing delivery is through shared collection development that attempts to place a given item at the academic institution where it is most likely to be used. So, for instance, if one university in a consortium specializes in astrophysics, that institution's library would by agreement build a comprehensive collection in that subject discipline for the entire consortium. Cooperative collection development has the interesting effect of reducing deliveries by concentrating materials where they are most likely to be used while simultaneously increasing the potential for more deliveries because this wise use of financial resources has increased the resource pool available to every patron in the consortium.

The larger systems are sorting ten, twenty, even thirty thousand items a day. These operations are labor intensive and expensive and have created a need for highly efficient manual sorting or automated material handling systems. New technology is available, for hefty price tags, which can sort and deliver to the correct location up to two thousand items an hour.

Technology also affects delivery in several ways. Libraries have long used electronic delivery for journal articles and short reports. New technologies, such as print-on-demand, downloadable e-books, and digitized books are beginning to affect physical delivery. Digitized books are another paradox for the delivery manager. An online book both increases and decreases the likelihood of an item needing delivery. If the item is available in electronic form, in principle it does not require delivery, since the patron can read it online. On the other hand, with digitized publications the actual contents of a monograph are searchable, revealing much more information about any given book. So it is likely that more researchers will find information of interest in that book and may want to see the entire monograph, thereby increasing delivery. A delivery manager often is juggling competing demands and interests, all of which add tension and complexity to the job.

MANAGING THE COURIER SERVICE

Whether an organization outsources its delivery system or maintains a fleet of trucks, it must build and maintain communications and relationships with participating libraries. Managing a delivery system is much like managing a library; there are issues related to contracts, personnel, budgets, and operations that require specialized knowledge. Communication technology is critical to the success of a complex delivery service. In addition to communication, a manager must deal with staffing, training, manuals, websites, contracts, conflicts, and other management issues.

It cannot be overstressed how critical communication is in managing a delivery service. Because of the complex nature of physical delivery services with multiple participants and often millions of items in transit, the potential for problems and misunderstandings is huge. Communication is hampered by the fact that most delivery services are not part of the library's internal communication network. Information about weather delays, route changes, pricing changes, code changes, and other key issues must be communicated to the proper person within the participating library. Without a robust communication network, problems can multiply and clog an entire system, reducing efficiency and increasing errors. In this book we go into detail on some of the best ways of keeping participating libraries informed, such as user committees, websites, manuals, and electronic information services.

A courier service must follow all the normal business practices. Mission statements, organizational goals, employee evaluations, and service evaluations are all must-do standard practices. When direct billing is required of participant libraries, best accounting practices must be followed. Courier managers often forget that marketing and public relations materials need to be developed and distributed even if there is a perception that participating libraries are a captive audience. Basically, if the courier manager does not tell the story of the courier service, someone else will define it in ways perhaps not in the best interest of the service. In times of financial cutback, a long-established, proactive marketing approach may pay huge dividends to the courier manager.

NEW TRENDS AND TECHNOLOGIES IN THE INDUSTRY

As mentioned at the beginning of this chapter, home delivery has always been a difficult subject for libraries. The difficulty has become exacerbated by changes in our culture related to social networking and Web 2.0 applications and by a new generation of patrons who are placing new service demands on libraries. Patrons want to find library materials quickly and on their own, and they want access now, not tomorrow. Librarians are often asked, why can't the library deliver books like Netflix and other Web 2.0 book and film exchange services?

The answer is that libraries can deliver to homes, and several public library systems and universities are doing just that. There are issues with cost, equipment, and policies that must be addressed in running a successful operation. These issues are all covered in this book. The problem is not in the application but in the mindset of today's librarian.

In public library systems that have home delivery, patron evaluations always place home delivery at the top of patron service preferences. Additionally, the overall cost of home delivery is typically equal to the cost of running a medium-sized branch library. So why aren't more libraries doing home delivery and building fewer brick-and-mortar branches? Why are there still only a few library systems doing home delivery when it so popular with patrons? This is an issue that the library community must confront in the next few years if we are to remain a viable service entity in our ever-changing communities.

Overall, library delivery managers have developed solid fundamentals for managing physical delivery services. New trends and techniques are revolutionizing delivery in parts of the country. These trends need to be shared to gained national attention. For instance, the final chapter in this book, on linking courier services, raises an interesting question about how libraries choose to spend their funds.

OCLC provides roughly ten million ILL transactions a year. For the sake of argument, let's make a few assumptions. Let's err on the conservative side and say that 50 percent of all ILL transactions are being sent by USPS between libraries. A 13-ounce book ships via USPS Media Mail with packaging and labor for around $3.50 one way or $7.00 round-trip. That means libraries are spending $35 million to ship OCLC ILL items through the USPS each year, estimated conservatively. Surely there must be less-expensive alternatives.

2

Factors Influencing Delivery Options

Valerie Horton and Brenda Bailey-Hainer

As mentioned in chapter 1, there are a variety of ways to categorize physical delivery. In this chapter we focus on how cost and speed of delivery affect the decisions to choose one of the four main delivery methods: USPS, commercial overnight carriers, in-house operations, and regional carriers. In chapter 3 we examine delivery systems organized from a library system or consortium focus—that is, whether the system is focusing on branch, regional, state, or multistate delivery.

A LIBRARY DELIVERY SURVEY

Libraries have long been dedicated to the concept of resource sharing, generously loaning their materials to other libraries. Over the years, many improvements have been made to resource sharing, making it faster and easier to borrow and lend materials. Some of the improvements have been to the requesting process itself. Unlike early resource-sharing efforts, now through library technology and the Internet the locations of millions of items are known and the requesting process has been simplified and made directly available to patrons.

Other improvements have been made in the automation of the requesting process, particularly by consortia. Circulation-based automated resource-sharing systems allow end users to place their own requests as circulation holds, called *direct consortium borrowing*. These systems have been a major factor in the skyrocketing ILL numbers. According to the National Center for Educational Statistics, academic libraries in 2006 loaned more than ten million items to other institutions.[1] Public libraries in 2005 borrowed around 36,000,000 items.[2]

Two systems illustrate the rapid rate of interlibrary growth that can be found throughout the country. MINITEX manages a statewide ILL system, MnLink, for Minnesota and the Dakotas. MnLink had an increase in ILL transactions from 100,000 in 2004 to more than 500,000 in 2007. Colorado supports several consortia and a statewide ILL system. Colorado had 282,672 ILL requests in 2003. By 2008, that number had risen to more than 700,000. Go to any consortium or statewide system in the country and you will find similar increases, particularly if patron direct borrowing is enabled.

Most consortium-based borrowing systems automatically perform load leveling, ensuring that all libraries share an even number of borrows and loans. The hold for the patron is placed only where the material shows as being available on the shelf at the owning institution, and the task of pulling the material is then delegated to circulation pages. These types of systems have shortened the time from request to fulfillment while significantly reducing costs.

Resources are becoming increasingly available electronically through such projects as Google Book Search and the Internet Archive. Because of copyright restrictions, only materials published prior to 1923 are widely available in digitized format. However, not all end users are ready to receive materials in electronic fashion. Although electronic resource delivery is expanding, it will still likely be five to ten years before a critical mass of materials is available in electronic form and before the majority of the public is ready to receive everything they want in electronic form.

In the meantime, the primary method for sharing many library materials is still to ship the item physically from point A to point B. Often this is done via a dedicated delivery network, which we refer to as a *library courier* throughout this book. These systems are pervasive throughout the country, and it is difficult to name all of them definitively. What we do know is that they are numerous and all share some basic characteristics.

To place the delivery models in context, it helps to understand the current state of delivery in the United States. In the remainder of this section we focus on the first major library physical delivery survey ever conducted, in April and

May 2008 by Brenda Bailey-Hainer, Valerie Horton, Greg Pronevitz, and Melissa Stockton. Delivery managers from around the country responded to a lengthy questionnaire covering a wide range of issues from pricing to delivery schedules to vendor relations. The survey was designed to provide a snapshot into the current landscape of physical delivery for U.S. libraries.

Unlike an on-demand, commercial delivery service such as that offered by UPS or FedEx, which make pickups and deliveries on an as-needed basis, library couriers tend to have a set route with scheduled stops at specific times at specific libraries on specific days of the week. The courier automatically stops at each scheduled location regardless of whether there is material to pick up or drop off. Totes, bins, canvas or plastic bags, cardboard mailers, boxes, and even plastic milk-type cartons are used to move items between scheduled stops.

Library courier delivery services are often managed by consortia, such as independent 501(c)(3) organizations, regional library systems or cooperatives of libraries, state library agencies, public libraries with multiple branches, or academic institutions with multiple campuses. In many instances, these organizations contract with a commercial carrier to provide the service. In those cases, the carrier is usually handling multiple contracts on the same route. For example, the courier may stop not only at libraries but also at other locations to drop off or pick up pharmaceuticals, cancelled checks, or developed film. In other cases, the managing organization may own its own fleet of delivery vehicles and hire its own drivers, essentially running the operation in-house. Several use a combination of both a commercial carrier and an in-house fleet.

Consortia running delivery services may represent a single type (e.g., academic) or be multitype, with any combination of public, academic, school, or special libraries participating. Statewide implementations that cover all types of libraries tend to be the largest and most heavily used among library couriers, with some serving more than 1,100 libraries and delivering more than ten million items annually. In this survey, however, most library delivery services tended to be smaller and regional based.

Responses to the survey came from thirty states: Alabama, Arizona, California, Colorado, Connecticut, Delaware, Florida, Georgia, Illinois, Indiana, Kansas, Louisiana, Massachusetts, Maryland, Maine, Michigan, Minnesota, Missouri, North Carolina, New Jersey, New York, Ohio, Oregon, Pennsylvania, Rhode Island, South Dakota, Texas, Virginia, Washington, and Wisconsin. Additionally, anecdotal evidence suggests that almost all of the lower forty-eight states have one or more library couriers in operation within their state boundaries delivering to a least a few major libraries.

The survey found that fees libraries pay for courier service are determined in different ways. Some couriers are partially subsidized with either state (more than 70 percent) or federal funding (more than 13 percent); others benefit from local support such as county or library district tax revenue. In some cases, the overall cost of the courier is shared by participating libraries. This annual cost per library may be calculated through a per-stop cost, the volume of materials moved, indirectly paid for as part of an overall membership fee in an organization, or some combination of these methods. Often there is a flat fee for the year, but it may be based on some type of hierarchical pricing structure.

As the price of fuel has risen dramatically in recent years, a provision for a gasoline surcharge tied to the relevant average state price for gasoline is increasingly prevalent in contracts between libraries and commercial carriers. If the cost of gas increases above a specified price during the contract year, this cost may be passed on to libraries. According to survey, the total cost for operating the courier ranges from $1,100 to $2.25 million annually, reflecting both the smallest and largest operations.

Delivery is still for the most part restricted to Monday through Friday, though at least eleven couriers in the United States have Saturday delivery and one courier also offers delivery on Sunday. Twelve of the couriers responding to the survey reported that they support deliveries more than once per day; typically these are public library systems that deliver to their own branches and then deliver to other unaffiliated libraries in the area.

For organizations that outsource their delivery, most report that they have had an ongoing relationship with their commercial carrier. Only 9 percent reported that they had been with their courier less than one year, 50 percent one to three years, and 42 percent three or more years. This confirms many anecdotes that suggest how uneven commercial carrier distribution is across the country. Indeed, in some states, like Idaho, despite putting together a "dating" profile to attract couriers to their state, there is no single courier that can serve the entire state in a cost-effective manner. Other sparsely populated Western states with huge geographic areas have found it more affordable and convenient to use the USPS instead of a dedicated library courier.

The delivery sector has instituted many improvements to keep costs low. For instance, some couriers use automated sorting systems and preprinted delivery labels, which have helped reduce the number of erroneously delivered packages and other errors. Surprisingly, at least seven courier systems still use entirely handwritten routing labels, and very few have incorporated bar codes or RFID tags into the sorting process. In many ways, physical delivery has continued to be a primarily manual process. Sorting is handled most frequently on the route by the driver, at a single sorting facility, or at regional sorting centers.

With many different delivery systems crisscrossing the country, it is not surprising that many of the couriers connect with other systems. Of the survey respondents, fifty-six couriers indicated that they connected to another library courier system; this might be connections between a multibranch public library system courier and a surrounding suburban library system or between a regional courier and a statewide courier.

Most organizations gather some type of statistics to help measure efficiency, reliability, and satisfaction level with their courier service. The most commonly kept statistics are the volume of items delivered (59 percent), volume by bin or container (44 percent), and turnaround time for point-to-point delivery (21 percent).

As the demand by participating libraries for convenience increases, courier services have increased their special services. Three couriers reported supporting home delivery, 8 percent reported special handling of archival or rare materials, and twenty-nine services handled nonstandard materials such as AV equipment or library supplies. On-demand deliveries allow a cost-effective balance between regular service for high-volume institutions and those that require infrequent delivery options.

Whatever the options offered by a local courier service to its customers, it is clear that libraries will continue to take advantage of the cost-effective option of a library courier service until universal electronic delivery of materials becomes a reality.

THE IMPACT OF COSTS AND SPEED IN CHOOSING A DELIVERY PROVIDER

The just-mentioned survey found that the physical delivery of library materials is widespread, if unevenly distributed, throughout the country. The widespread use of library delivery services demonstrates their importance to libraries. The survey also illustrates the different models used by library delivery services. There are many different types of delivery services available to a library or consortium, each developed in relative isolation and reflecting the unique character of the region it serves.

Every region has unique topography and political characteristics that influence the development of the library delivery service. For instance, some states have robust regional library systems, like Massachusetts or California, which chose to connect independent library delivery services to create a statewide network. In other states, like Maine and Louisiana, the state library provides delivery, though often only to public libraries. A common model is for an existing consortium to create a physical delivery service as an additional service to its members in support of a global catalog function.

Geography also plays a role in delivery development. Driving distances per route in a relatively small, flat state like Rhode Island (1,545 square miles) is very different from those in Colorado, with its mountain passes and 100,000 square miles. The political situation also affects how courier services are formed. Each state, region, or consortium has its own unique circumstance and membership. For instance, research-oriented academic institutions are often more interested in speed over cost and tend to favor using the commercial overnight services like FedEx.

Given that physical delivery services represent the unique character of their region and member needs, it is not surprising that there is a wide range of delivery services. Among all the factors influencing delivery decisions, two have the most impact—cost and speed of delivery. ILL departments have become sophisticated at choosing the best delivery method for each transaction they handle. Usually, the least expensive option is the first choice, but for some consortia, particularly in high-end science or medical fields, time is more important than cost. The more delivery options available to a library, the better it can serve its patrons. A sample matrix might include the following options:

- OCLC request—if in region use local courier; if out of state use USPS
- consortium request—use local courier
- medical research consortium—use consortium's negotiated FedEx rate
- international request—use FedEx or UPS

The costs for shipping ILL from several Colorado libraries illustrate the difference price makes. Large public libraries spend as little as 25 cents per in-state courier transaction, whereas those that ship fewer items pay more, up to a dollar per transaction. One of the largest universities in Colorado reports spending $5,604 on USPS, $36,206 on FedEx, and $13,302 on UPS in one year. A large public library in Colorado reported spending more than $50,000 each year on USPS-shipped ILL. ILL shipping can be expensive, and library staff will choose the least expensive option that meets their delivery needs.

Below we review each of the four primary delivery options and how cost and speed influence the selection and development of delivery.

United States Post Office

The longest-running and most widely used method of physical delivery of library materials has been the USPS. Traditional ILL service and the USPS mail have long been linked together, and the mail is still commonly used for interstate and international interlibrary transactions. The history and volume of library items moved by the USPS make it the de facto standard from which all other delivery methods are compared.

There are several different rates used by USPS, for Media Mail, Parcel Post, First Class, and so forth. The least expensive rate for an item weighing less than 13 ounces (about the size of a large paperback) is Media Mail. A regular-sized paperback ships for under $2.40 by Media Mail; USPS Priority Mail and Parcel Post are more expensive.

Media Mail is commonly used in libraries for books, film, manuscripts, printed music, sound recordings, play scripts, charts, binders, videotapes, and computer-recorded media such as CDs. The maximum size of a box shipped is 108 inches (length plus girth). Pricing is based on weight. Packages weighing more than one pound must be shipped directly from the post office. Costs are incurred in both shipping and returning the item.

Although the USPS claims that it delivers Media Mail in seven business days, ILL staff frequently tell borrowers that delivery can take as long as two weeks. Further, packing requirements are quite specific: "Choose a box with enough room for cushioning material around the contents. Sturdy paperboard or corrugated fiberboard boxes are best for weights up to 10 pounds" or "Place the cushioning all around your item or items. You can use newspaper, foam peanuts, or shredded paper."[3]

USPS packaging requirements add considerably to cost and labor. It can take three to five minutes to wrap a packing for mailing, depending on size. Packing time can become a major staff labor cost, particularly if numerous packages are mailed each day, and there are additional costs for packaging materials. Although the USPS is generally reliable, lost items are not reimbursed unless one of several confirmation or tracking features is purchased. These tracking services add considerable time and cost to each delivery and so are seldom used by libraries.

The major strengths of USPS are that it is everywhere, it is trustworthy, and the prices are relatively inexpensive. Its two main disadvantages are slow delivery times and costly packaging and labor costs, which can be significant barriers to high-quality patron services.

Commercial Overnight Delivery

Nationwide commercial delivery from UPS and FedEx are also commonly used by libraries. These services have several powerful advantages including speed, name recognition, reliability, and almost universal availability. Other advantages of overnight carriers include their professional, well-trained drivers and the fact that they visit many libraries routinely to deliver new acquisitions. Because they have individual package tracking, they are quick to reimburse for lost materials. On the negative side, delivery is not universal, since these commercial carriers do not go to every rural location or deliver to USPS addresses such as post office boxes.

Commercial carriers are used for all types of library delivery services, but they are most commonly used when speed is critical. The most common application is for medical, scientific, and legal consortia with a need for delivery overnight. Researchers often need materials as fast as possible. Universities also have found that some of their more valuable materials are better safeguarded with the package tracking features built into the commercial carrier system.

The main problem with overnight carriers is cost. An informal study I (V.H.) conducted in 2008 of a dozen consortia that use commercial carriers found that pricing per package ranged from around $4.50 to $10.90. In 2007 a Library Research Service (LRS) study was conducted of twenty-seven academic, public, school, and special libraries for one week's worth of deliveries. Counts were taken of items delivered through a local courier service, and those counts where compared to shipments made via the USPS, UPS, and FedEx.[4] The library courier cost for one week was $2,343, the USPS cost $10,341, the UPS cost $17,641, and the FedEx cost $18,269. This LRS study clearly demonstrates that commercial carriers are far more expensive than either a library delivery service or the USPS.

The LRS study used published pricing to make the comparisons. However, pricing for commercial carriers varies significantly by contract. One consortium revealed that it had been paying the same price for fifteen years with no price increases. Other overnight carrier contracts have built-in annual price increases. Since each delivery service negotiates its own contracts with the national carriers, there is room for rather astonishing differences in service and price.

Like the USPS, another negative associated with nationwide carriers can be packaging time and material costs. Even if the service provides the mailing envelopes, time is still required to pack the shipment and fill out paperwork. Most libraries do not have time to track an individual item once it is en route and use this part of the service only when an item is missing. Further, the commercial carrier pricing models include significant price increases as weight increases. The distance traveled also increases cost, particularly for items that cross one of the service's self-defined regions. All of this makes predicting delivery costs difficult for libraries using commercial overnight carriers.

Delivery managers have found that nationwide carriers often will not bid on a library delivery proposal request. The library market is not the primary market for commercial services, though there are exceptions. In 2008, Brooklyn Public Library contracted with UPS to take over their internal branch delivery. This suggests that members of the logistics industry are trying to be flexible in meeting delivery demands in a difficult market and may be more receptive to library contracts in the future.

Given the cost a library pays for speedy delivery, commercial carriers are often limited to those systems that move relatively few items a year—in the low tens of thousands at best. Pennsylvania is using UPS to ship 500,000 items each year, and that is likely about as large as that service could grow given the costs involved. No library courier service that moves over a million items a year is using a nationwide commercial carrier as a primary service system. High costs always limit the amount of delivery growth, and this is a major service disadvantage to library patrons.

Contracting with Regional and Local Carriers

The marketplace for regional and local carriers is both widespread and highly regionalized. In 2002, the U.S. Census Bureau identified 12,754 couriers and messengers services.[5] There are regional carriers that do business through most of the United States and some that operate only within a few city blocks. Some regional carriers have become large corporations, and others remain run by one person. Libraries have contracted with all types of regional carriers to meet unique local needs. What all regional carriers must be is faster and cheaper than the USPS.

An example of a larger regional carrier is Lanter Delivery Systems, which has contracts with numerous library systems and does business in all but about a dozen states. The Association of Southeastern Research Libraries uses Lanter to deliver to twelve universities in ten states. There are other regional carriers who also market directly to libraries, including R. R. Donnelly, Edge Logistics, and Velocity Express; all three cover large regions of the country.

There are also many regional carriers that serve a smaller set of states. American Courier delivers to Wyoming, South Dakota, Nebraska, Iowa, and Colorado. First Choice Courier delivers to Missouri, Illinois, and Kansas. The advantage to libraries that sign up with the smaller regional carriers is that a more geographically centered carrier is more likely to understand local circumstances, such as which mountain passes are best avoided in winter. These regional carriers tend to employee local drivers who can build relationships with participating libraries.

On the other side of the scale, there is a small delivery service in Orange County, Florida, that has only one client—the Orange County library system. This company and the library have successfully operated a branch delivery and home delivery service for more than twenty years (see chapter 11).

For libraries or consortia that do not want to run their own internal fleet or hire drivers, a regional carrier has advantages. Most regional carriers provide "conjunctive deliveries" (shared deliveries) with pharmacies, financial institutions, film developers, office suppliers, and the like. This keeps prices low, since the library pays only for part of the material shipped in each truck or van.

The regional carrier market is volatile, with companies opening in good economic times and going out of business in bad. This market volatility has left consortia without delivery service. In Kansas in the 1990s, the library's delivery company went out of business quite suddenly and the state's librarians were unable to find another company to provide delivery. In Colorado when the same thing occurred, the consortium that manages the state's delivery service was able to find another provider within a few days. Whether it is easy or hard to find a new regional carrier, the disruption of service and changes required by joining a new service are negatives for choosing regional carriers.

Regional carriers are usually less expensive per item delivered than the USPS. If a consortium has a set fee, the price for each item sent from a larger library system can be pennies on the dollar. Regional carriers are generally fast. Many typically provide overnight or two-day delivery. This timeliness is contingent on having delivery five days a week; if the courier picks up and delivers only two or three days a week, the speed of the entire service is compromised. Regional carriers are a popular option among library delivery services. Overall, they beat the USPS in speed and cost. More information on regional carriers can be found in chapters 5 and 6.

In-House Delivery Services

In-house delivery systems typically develop when a large public or regional library system decides to expand to include delivery to nearby suburban libraries. From there it can be very cost-effective to continue to expand delivery to ever-wider circles, until the entire state is receiving coverage. The South Central Library System of Madison, Wisconsin, is a statewide service that started delivering to the libraries in a four-county region and now delivers more than one and a half million items statewide. If a library system is already maintaining a fleet of trucks and drivers, the overhead costs of having a repair shop in-house, negotiating fuel contracts, and driver salaries are all expandable at a much lower cost than with a start-up business.

The advantage of in-house delivery is the control over the routes run and the times of delivery. A larger central library can receive delivery several times a day, whereas the smaller libraries in rural areas need less delivery. There are also advantages to having drivers who are in-house employees rather than subcontractors with a commercial service. If the drivers are employees, they are more likely to be committed to the service and understand the culture of libraries they regularly visit.

The disadvantage of in-house systems is that, since the library service has control, it also has responsibility for delivery. If a driver does not show up, it is not uncommon for a library manager, or even a library director, to have to drive a route. It can also be difficult to determine the exact cost of delivery per piece, for much of the cost is tied into the main public library's branch delivery network. How do you determine the cost of support for the larger city public library and for statewide delivery when all are sharing the same resources?

Overall, in-house delivery is much faster than USPS delivery. Like regional carrier delivery, most items are delivered in a day or less, and for larger libraries multiple daily deliveries are possible. Delivery is cheaper than with the USPS, though no studies have confirmed by exactly how much. In-house delivery is popular for regional delivery where costs and distance driven can be controlled. More information on in-house delivery can be found in chapter 4.

ISSUES WITH DELIVERY TO LOW-VOLUME LIBRARIES

How do you arrange cost-effective delivery to libraries that borrow or loan only a few items a month? This question plagues courier managers. Larger library systems that make up the bulk of a state's interlibrary traffic want to put everything on the state's courier. They do not want to deal with the labor associated with packaging for USPS delivery. In any delivery service, where the goal is to reach all the libraries in a given region or state, the issue of small libraries must be solved. Different courier systems have developed different solutions.

Colorado attempts to have delivery to every one of its libraries. In a recent study, the majority of the small libraries had no ILL activities during the period studied and those libraries that did borrow materials averaged only one or two items a month. More correspondence was shared with the smaller libraries than interlibrary materials. With so little activity, it cannot be cost-effective to send a driver to the remote parts of the service regions where many of the smallest libraries are found.

A seemingly logical solution is to use the USPS in such cases, and many systems do just that. As noted earlier, the problem with the USPS is that Media Mail delivery can take seven to ten business days, and with packaging and labor the cost can mount up quickly. In Colorado, many of the large libraries mail only to in-state libraries. If a library is not on the courier, it does not get ILL requests fulfilled.

Colorado's solution is to use a "community stop" model. In this model, one library serves as a hub for smaller libraries. For example, in a community of five thousand people, the public library may have delivery five days a week. The school and the museum library staff drive to the public library to pick up and drop off any ILL transactions they have. The library courier makes one stop, and so time is managed efficiently.

A more common solution is to use an overnight commercial carrier for the smallest libraries. MINITEX and several states use this option. For a handful of small library requests, the items are sent to a main sorting facility and packaged for UPS delivery. This has the advantage of keeping items moving through the system quickly, though with a hefty price per package. This solution does not work everywhere, for the commercial carriers do not deliver to every rural area in many states.

Unfortunately, in too many cases small libraries are simply out of luck. They cannot afford to be part of a courier system, and they may suffer because of large libraries that are overspending their mailing budgets and unwilling to ship to these locations. The delivery community continues to study the problem of small libraries, seeking a better alternative.

Notes

1. Barbara Holton, Laura Hardesty, and Patricia O'Shea, *Academic Libraries: 2006 First Look,* NCES 2008-337 (U.S. Department of Education, National Center for Education Statistics, 2008).
2. Adrienne Chute and P. Elaine Kroe, *Public Libraries in the United States: Fiscal Year 2005,* NCES 2008-301 (U.S. Department of Education, National Center for Education Statistics, 2007).

3. United States Post Office, "Preparing Packages" (2008), http://pe.usps.com/text/dmm100/preparing.htm.

4. Zeth Lietzau, *Statewide Courier Saves Libraries Thousands in Shipping Costs Each Year,* ED3/110.10/No. 251 (Library Research Service, Colorado State Library, Colorado Department of Education, 2007).

5. U.S. Census Bureau, *Couriers and Messengers: 2002 Economic Census.* EC02-481-06 (U.S. Department of Commerce, Economics and Statistics Administration, 2004).

3

Physical Delivery Service Organization

Bruce Smith

Library physical delivery service models come in all shapes and sizes. Many delivery services have developed out of local library organizations and regional sharing agreements. Statewide and interstate library delivery networks often were created because they were the most cost-efficient and effective shipping option to support expanded resource sharing between libraries outside of their local library system or resource-sharing consortium. In this chapter we provide a broad explanation of how libraries are typically connected to each other through delivery and which delivery models are frequently employed for the various service areas. Our focus here is on courier-based models rather than more ubiquitous package delivery services offered by the likes of the USPS, UPS, and FedEx.

We distinguish four main organizational models of library delivery service—local branch, intrastate regional system or consortium, statewide, and interstate or cross-border—but it is not uncommon for a given library to be served by many types of delivery services working together behind the scene. At times, a resource-sharing item travels through all four models to reach its destination.

BRANCH LIBRARY ORGANIZATIONS

Library-to-library delivery as we know it today had its beginnings in county or municipal branch public library systems and at larger universities with multiple campus libraries. Whether moving materials between branch locations to fill item requests or to shift floating bulk collections between branches, a regular delivery service is required to provide similar services to all patrons. Since the entire organization is under one budget, determining delivery service levels and how the service is managed and implemented is not dependent on agreements with other libraries, systems, or consortia.

The most common approach with this level of local branch service is for the library organization to manage and operate in-house. Depending on the volume shipped between locations, the delivery service may be dedicated, meaning vehicles and drivers are employed specifically to handle only the delivery of library material between branches. Alternatively, it may delegate the service as a duty to be performed by another department such as maintenance services or a campus motor pool. Because of these organizations' size, establishing delivery between branches as an in-house service is typically feasible and most cost-effective.

Some organizations with branches do outsource either the delivery service, the centralized sorting, or both. Recently, the Brooklyn Public Library system contracted with UPS to be their delivery service between their branches. Library delivery managers are creative in finding partners and cost-effective delivery solutions. Decisions about whether to operate an in-house delivery service or to contract with a private courier are frequently based on cost and the capabilities of an organization to operate a delivery service in terms of staff and space available. See chapters 4 and 5 for a more thorough investigation of the pro and cons of in-house versus contractual delivery.

INTRASTATE REGIONAL LIBRARY SYSTEMS AND CONSORTIA

Often independent libraries are a part of governmentally created regional library service systems based on geographic boundaries or are members of a consortium of libraries in a particular region. These systems and consortia may consist of either a single type of library such as a public library system, or they can comprise multiple types of libraries. Although systems and consortia offer their members many services, most offer libraries the ability to share materials among themselves easily via ILL requests or direct patron requests from a shared union catalog. When this level of sharing is created, the system or consortium must also create a physical delivery service to support regional borrowing and lending.

System or consortium delivery service is typically funded in one of three ways: by the system or consortium, by fees from the member libraries, or by a combination of the two sources. Funding levels can be based on numerous factors, but they often take into account the frequency or volume of service.

Delivery services to libraries in a system or consortium can be operated in-house or outsourced to a private courier. Any required centralized sorting can also be handled by either the system or a private courier. Sometimes there is a hybrid of delivery services within a system or consortium. A system member may be a municipal or county branch library organization that receives delivery from the consortium at its main library location but handles all deliveries to its own branches with its own delivery service. However, some systems serve all libraries and branches directly through the system delivery service.

STATEWIDE LIBRARY DELIVERY NETWORKS

Statewide library delivery networks can function as consolidated services, connecting directly to all the libraries participating in the statewide delivery network. Alternatively, they can be organized as a hub-and-spoke organization with a main framework of delivery routes (spokes) connecting to the headquarters (hubs) of local regional delivery services to exchange intersystem or consortium materials (see figure 3.1). Often the structure of a statewide delivery network is a combination of libraries being directly served by statewide routes and some libraries being connected to the statewide network through their regional system or consortium delivery service hub.

Funding for statewide library delivery services happens in many different fashions. Most are either fully or partially funded by the state. Some are subsidized with available state library grant funding or through federal grants. Many statewide delivery services are partially or fully funded by their participants, either by a system group, such as a university paying for service to all its campus libraries, or by individual participating libraries.

The common practice is for statewide delivery service to be contracted out to private carrier companies. This makes sense for several reasons, the main being cost. Because of driving distances and a lower level of volume transported on a statewide level, contracting with a private courier allows the service to receive conjunctive route service pricing. A private courier is more than likely to have

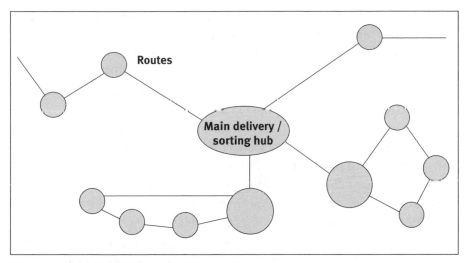

Figure 3.1   Hub-and-spoke delivery model

other delivery business in the same areas as the libraries in the delivery network, which allows cost sharing.

For example, Wisconsin operates a hybrid statewide delivery service. One of Wisconsin's public library regional systems provides an in-house delivery service to the majority of the state. In the Madison area, where volume is high, an in-house operation is the most cost-effective. Since interstate volume is not at the same level, it is more cost-effective to serve these parts of the state by contracting out to a commercial carrier. Managing a hybrid service, whether a combination of in-house and private courier or a combination of different private courier vendors, has the advantage of providing service stability should a particular vendor no longer be a viable option.

LIBRARY DELIVERY ACROSS STATE BORDERS

Interstate library delivery that crosses state borders comes in two forms: either it is the function of a library consortium with membership from multiple states, or it is the result of two or more statewide delivery networks or consortia making a delivery connection between their delivery hubs.

Several consortia around the country offer their services to libraries across state borders. Like statewide delivery networks, the most cost-efficient and effective manner to provide the service is typically contracting with a private courier that operates in the states served. The delivery service model could also be a hybrid model with a combination of an in-house delivery service and private courier forming the delivery network or a combination of different private courier vendors. Service funding is most commonly either included in the membership fees of the consortium or paid for by separate delivery service fees based on factors such as delivery frequency and volume.

An example of a multistate consortium managing library delivery services is the Committee on Institutional Cooperation (CIC), a consortium of the Big Ten universities plus the University of Chicago. This consortium's delivery service logistics are managed by a third-party logistics company that subcontracts routes to various private couriers spanning from Minneapolis, Minnesota, to Happy Valley, Pennsylvania. Other examples are the Orbis Cascade Alliance, which manages delivery service to libraries in Oregon, Washington, and Idaho, and Amigos Library Services, which has membership in Arkansas, Oklahoma, Texas, New Mexico, and Arizona.

An example of two or more separate statewide delivery networks connecting to each other is the partnership between MINITEX, based in Minneapolis, and the Wisconsin Libraries' Delivery Network based in Madison. MINITEX coordinates a multistate delivery network for the states of Minnesota, North Dakota, and South Dakota, and the Wisconsin network serves only that state. The delivery connection between the two delivery hubs is contracted with the private courier that provides the delivery connection for the CIC between the University of Minnesota and the University of Wisconsin. The contract cost is shared equally between MINITEX and the State of Wisconsin's Reference and Loan Library. There is also a reciprocal borrowing agreement between the two to facilitate the exchange of materials.

Part Two

Library Delivery
Service Models

4
Creating an In-House Delivery System

Bruce Smith

One of the questions many library organizations ask themselves when discussing library delivery is, should we be doing it ourselves? To determine whether running an in-house service could be advantageous, a library system must know what level of volume it is handling in library-to-library delivery transfers within its system. The two main options for handling deliveries are dedicated routes and conjunctive routes.

A dedicated route makes sense when (1) the total volume handled at the various libraries served by a route maximizes the capacity of the vehicle according to space or weight limitations, and (2) the libraries on the route are within a geographic region that allows the route to be driven within reasonable time and mileage limitations. One of the primary situations better served by outsourcing delivery is when a library system has low volume to deliver over a longer distance. It is expensive to send a mostly empty vehicle and driver to make such an exchange. A private courier can handle such a stop as conjunctive business—loading the library material onto a vehicle already making other deliveries such as film, banking records, or pharmaceuticals to the same destination area.

IS A DEDICATED ROUTE PRACTICAL?

Whether a dedicated route is practical depends on the volume handled, route configurations, and the needed frequency of service.

Determining Volume Handled

Material volume data for delivery planning must be summarized by each day of the week and by both the volume dropped off and the volume picked up at each library.

Using ILL statistics is one quick method to determine delivery volume, but these data do not accurately capture the true volume shipped between libraries and can be difficult to break down by days of the week. Many items that are sent between libraries are not counted in ILL statistics, such as damaged item returns to owning libraries, courtesy returns, interdepartmental mail, and book sale materials, to name a few. ILL counts do, however, provide a figure sufficient for determining potential for a dedicated route service.

To make that determination, ILL materials both sent and received by a location must be counted. Added together, these two provide a ballpark figure of the number of items shipped and received by a library. If only loans sent are counted, that number needs to be doubled, since all items loaned must come home. But with this method the volume may be skewed, since the library may be a net lender or a net borrower.

A better counting method is to have each library count each item it sends out and receives each day of the week. This not only captures all types of materials shipped but also indicates volume by each day of the week. This information can be used to determine how much space a library's delivery materials will occupy in a vehicle, which is needed for structuring potential routes.

To get a more accurate picture of delivery volume over the course of a year, it is best to perform hand counts at least three times per year: early spring, midsummer, and late fall. These periods coincide with school calendars. Performing this data collection over time provides growth patterns by library, which aids long-range planning for either an in-house dedicated route service or a courier conjunctive route. This information also assists library staff with space and staff planning.

Route Configurations

After per-library delivery volume data are gathered, potential route planning can begin to determine if dedicated route service is an option. This can be done in a variety of ways, but the easiest is to use simple mapping software (e.g., Microsoft Streets and Trips) or web based trip planning (e.g., Google Maps or MapQuest). Use the route-planning function of the mapping program and begin adding stop locations to the route planner. As this is done, track which libraries are added to the planner along with each library's delivery volume (both incoming and outgoing) from the library's highest volume day of the week.

Group libraries that are in the same region in order to begin configuring a route. As libraries are added, using the "get directions" function provides time and mileage estimates. Each area of the country has unique geography and traffic, so there is no magic formula for deciding which length of route is reasonable in terms of time and mileage. Factors that must be considered include pre-route and post-route duties, elevation gains, rush hour traffic, material exchange time at libraries, and allotted break/lunch times.

Frequency of Service

The number of days per week service is provided is chosen on the basis of two criteria: desired transit time and volume of materials. Keep in mind, though, that having a courier, especially a low-cost service, can increase traffic over time as resource sharing proves itself to participating libraries. Increasing the number of delivery days improves the transit time of materials, ultimately improving service to patrons.

The volume component is simple: if the materials dropped off and picked up on a route overload the vehicle serving the route, either the vehicle size or the number of delivery days must be increased. Increased frequency also benefits both the library and central sorting location by spreading the workflow load out over more days and reducing the space needed to store incoming and outgoing materials.

The alternative to either larger vehicles or increased frequency is to create another delivery route to spread the volume over more routes. This option increases mileage and driver time expense and requires the purchase of an additional vehicle, but it does not improve patron service or increase any of the delivery locations' ability to handle incoming and outgoing volume, since each site still receives and sends the same daily volume. Typically, the cost of adding an extra day of service, in terms of time and mileage, is similar to that of adding a new route. The new route option does carry the additional capital expense of a new vehicle.

Once you determine your volume and find a reasonable route configuration, you can assess the practicality of dedicated service. Typical cargo vehicle load capacities fall in the payload classes of 1,000–2,000 pounds (standard cargo van), 4,000–5,000 pounds (14- to 16-foot cube/box truck), and 8,000–10,000 pounds (18- to 24-foot freight trucks). As a general rule of thumb, one item equals one pound.

ADVANTAGE OF IN-HOUSE SERVICE

Once delivery volume data are compiled, potential routes are configured, and dedicated route service is determined to be feasible, the question remains, what are the advantages of running an in-house service? It comes down to cost and control.

If the library volume is enough to fill a vehicle on its own, then the expense of managing delivery should be relatively similar for both a library-run service and a private courier. This leaves two expense variables that determine whether a library-run or private courier is more cost-effective—operational overhead and operational efficiency. Direct control over the service is the main factor in managing these variables.

A well-managed library-run service should be able to maintain operational administrative overhead costs as well as a private courier. Libraries already have much of the administrative business structure in place and, though the additional payroll and account management for a distribution service does add time and expense, the total expense of the department(s) handling this operational administration is tied in with the administration of other library business and services. The administration overhead for a courier that is not diversified in other businesses is a dedicated expense for a courier company.

Also, private couriers carry the additional overhead cost of salespeople. A salesperson's income usually consists of a base salary, which is an operational expense that must be built into pricing, and additional compensation based on sales.

Another overhead consideration is profit. Private courier companies, understandably, are in the business to make money.

The variable of operational efficiency is where control over the service can have a dramatic impact on costs. Libraries have a greater understanding of the processes involved in the resource-sharing supply chain. There are three main areas where efficiencies can be gained by a library-managed service.

1. *Library delivery material processing and centralized sorting* are best exemplified in the cases of two library systems. The Northeast Regional Library System in Massachusetts sorts for seventy-five member library locations. It contracts with a private courier to handle all sorting and delivery for the system. As delivery material volume has grown from patron use of their online shared catalog, the courier expense to sort the materials has grown.

As of 2007, the sending libraries do not separate materials going to the central sorting location in any manner. Thus, the courier has the seventy-five sorting locations on shelving units arranged alphabetically in a large square. In this setup, each sorter sorts 200–250 items per hour. The courier is not aware of the libraries' capabilities to separate outgoing materials, nor is it in its bottom line interest to determine what efficiencies are possible. A courier's cost factor is increased revenue, whereas the library system's is an increased budget expense.

Conversely, the South Central Library System (SCLS) in Wisconsin manages its own delivery and central sorting operation and has sixty-three member library sorting locations. SCLS has libraries send materials presorted into three different totes, allowing it to split up its central sorting area into three smaller areas. With sorting in smaller areas and to fewer locations in those areas, the sorting rate per sorter is 550–600 items per hour. Serving the system's interest first is possible through cooperative library and delivery planning.

Centralized sorting can also improve in-library handling of incoming delivery materials. At the central sorting location, materials can be separated to improve efficiency. One example is separating hold items from return items. Again, having a better understanding of internal library operations allows a library-managed service to make adaptations to improve efficiency.

2. *Handling more than ILL.* Private couriers can have surcharges for additional volume or include volume caps as part of their contract. With an in-house service, other types of delivery transfers can support the library, such as delivering different types of rotating collections (e.g., story kits, large-print materials, books on CD). Some services handle moving computer equipment for repair or rotating wireless laptop training labs. If the miles are already being traveled and space can be coordinated in the vehicles to handle additional transfers, the only cost effect is the minimal extra handling time it takes the driver. The same goes for a private courier, in that handling the occasional extra item does not increase

time and mileage, but the courier business is based on selling cargo capacity in their vehicles.

3. *Fleet planning.* The appropriate vehicles, in terms of maximizing capacity to handle high volume, are not always used by a courier, which can result in more driver time and mileage and, thus, higher costs to a library. This is especially the case with courier companies that employ independent contractors to provide the actual delivery, since most independent contractors typically must own their own vehicle.

For example, if a large cube truck can handle 150 typical totes according to space and weight, and a standard cargo van can handle only 50 totes, three separate routes using three cargo vehicles and three drivers would be needed to handle what could be done on one route with one truck and one driver. Not only are the single-route total mileage and driver time less than having to run three routes, they allow for better library service in terms of transit time. By having more libraries on a single route, more en route forwarding for same day delivery can occur. A larger vehicle is less fuel efficient, but this is more than offset by the additional driver time, mileage-related expenses, number of vehicles purchased, and insurance coverage of the three-route structure.

THE NUTS AND BOLTS OF AN IN-HOUSE DELIVERY SERVICE

The two main outlays of capital to begin a delivery service are for facility and fleet. The funding needed to establish one's own service prevents many library systems from considering anything but the private courier industry. But if an organization wants to control service, operational efficiencies, and ongoing costs, starting an in-house service may be its best option.

A delivery service must house both the fleet and central sorting. It must also have room to grow. Often a system may be able to provide space for central sorting within a current building and, if the system is smaller in size and does not need many vehicles, it may be able to handle parking easily in the same building or by renting nearby parking space. Ideally, whether large or small, vehicle parking and delivery sorting should be located in the same facility to limit labor expenses.

There are generally three options for vehicle purchasing: lease, buy new, or buy used. The advantage of leasing is that it spreads out the cost over time, but the overall cost of a leasing package ends up being higher than purchasing outright. Also, if the vehicle is to accumulate a high number of miles, there may be additional leasing costs.

In regards to purchasing, whether new or used, an important consideration is model similarity of vehicles in the fleet. Vehicle models tend to have similar maintenance issues over their lifetime. Closely tracking the fleet's maintenance history allows for preventative maintenance planning that can address potential problems that could occur at the most inopportune time—when a vehicle is on the road. Also, if vehicles are maintained according to manufacturer specifications and are kept until they are no longer safe to operate or their value is less than needed repairs, parts from a "dead" vehicle may be stripped for use on other similar models in the fleet. With a good preventative maintenance program, many commercial grade vehicles can have a life of 400,000 miles or more and ten or more years.

Purchasing a vehicle new is a good idea if the vehicle will be traveling a high number of miles per day. If, however, a vehicle will be used locally and not have a high number of miles, less than 25,000 miles per year, a used vehicle can save a great deal of up-front capital. Within the used truck market, the best option for finding a high-quality vehicle is purchasing from truck sales companies that deal in post-lease vehicles. Typically, leasing arrangements are set for three to five years and have maintenance plans built in. A three- to five-year-old vehicle will typically already have 90,000–120,000 miles on the odometer. The cost of a used 14- to 16-foot cube/box truck ranges between $15,000 and $20,000, compared to $38,000–$42,000 for a new vehicle in the same class. A good used vehicle should last for six to eight years, or approximately 300,000 miles, with a good maintenance program.

Because of extreme fuel market fluctuations, it is not feasible for us to advise on the different options. Gas, diesel, alternative fuel, electric, and fuel cell options all should be explored in depth as part of a purchasing decision.

STAFFING AND TRAINING

The demands on library delivery services have changed greatly in the past ten to twenty years. Online catalog access, patron direct borrowing, and increased patron knowledge of what is available have changed library delivery into a high-demand, high-volume business. The constant change in volume and expectations requires efficient and cost-effective delivery planning and execution.

The delivery manager is the key to achieving and maintaining high-quality delivery service. This person must be able to provide both detailed analysis and distribution solutions for service planning and day-to-day leadership, direction, and assistance to delivery staff and the libraries served. For this position, three or more years of supervisory experience in delivery systems or supply chain management should be required. Specific experience should be in capturing and analyzing material flow data, staff and service development, and customer service. For larger delivery systems, it is best to have assistant supervisors with similar qualifications. This is important for an organization's continuity in service and provides necessary supervisory backup.

Hiring driving staff is often a leap of faith. Drivers are trusted to operate vehicles safely. In addition, library materials are entrusted to drivers, and typically they also have keys and alarm access to libraries, which often are not open when the delivery is made. Because the liability and reputation of a library organization is at stake when hiring drivers, the hiring process of a driver should include much of the following: access to current driving record; criminal background search for bonding requirements; employment reference checks, especially for past driver jobs; road test in the vehicles the driver would be operating; and, depending on an organization's policies and any collective bargaining agreements, drug testing.

Drivers should receive all initial service orientation and route training by supervisory staff. This practice helps ensure that procedural information is provided to all new driving staff and improves the consistency in service provided to libraries. Follow-up training should be provided by supervisors as needed. Drivers should receive ongoing annual training in the areas of customer service, driving safety techniques, and proper material handling, especially related to lifting. A delivery procedures manual should be developed by the delivery service to provide a reference for staff throughout the year. This manual should be updated when changes are made and reviewed for needed revisions on a yearly basis.

Delivery management is responsible for determining the future needs of the delivery service. To provide this sort of planning, coordinators, managers, and supervisors must have an understanding of the trends in library resource sharing. In addition, staff in these positions should stay up to date on the standards, best practices, and innovations in material handling and distribution systems—those utilized not only in library delivery but in the general package courier and material handling industry. To do this, we recommend the following:

> Attend resource-sharing workshops that are relevant to library delivery systems. Attend state and national library conferences when they offer applicable programming.
>
> Access various trade associations and Internet and print resources that cover resource sharing and material handling:

- The Material Handling Industry of America typically covers the large warehousing industry but also provides information about material handling equipment for delivery and automated material handling.
- The Messenger Courier Association of the Americas is a group dedicated to the expedited package delivery industry. Members of this industry group most closely model library delivery systems and often provide delivery service for libraries.
- The Express Carriers Association is made up of regional carriers which, like Messenger Courier Association of the Americas members, currently provide delivery service for libraries.
- *Courier Magazine* is an online and print magazine dedicated to the courier industry.
- Library publications, specifically *Library Journal* and ALA's *American Libraries,* frequently have articles on resource sharing.
- The Moving Mountains Project and the Rethinking Resource Sharing Project are groups looking at all types of delivery models to improve patron service.

RISK MANAGEMENT AND LIABILITY

Whether an organization operates its own service or contracts with a private courier, there is a level of risk and liability associated with being in the delivery business. An advantage to contracting with a courier is that the library is not the first line of defense in a liability case. However, even with indemnification clauses in a courier contract, lawsuits still include all parties related to the business at hand.

When operating a library-managed service, additional insurance should be in place in case of a liability claim against a system's service. In addition to maintaining typical general liability insurance with $1 million in coverage, it is in a system's best interest to add umbrella liability coverage of $5 million or more. Also, since the delivery service is responsible for materials in its possession, an insurance bond should be in place that covers property loss.

The best coverage a system delivery service can have in place is in its own control. This boils down to hiring, training, and improving ergonomics and preventative maintenance. If proper vetting of potential drivers is done and staff are trained to a high degree, the risk of injury or accident can be greatly reduced. Also, it is important to improve material handling systems by adopting the best equipment suitable for the job. The risk of this business that most often becomes reality is on-the-job injury. Not only do employees deserve a safe working environment for their own well-being, the organization benefits from improved morale and fewer worker's compensation claims that cost the organization in both higher rates and loss of employee work time. Preventative maintenance of equipment and vehicles reduces the risk of injury or damage.

A practice that reduces theft potential for the libraries served is management of keys and access. Many couriers maintain keys and security codes to a building. All steps must be taken to ensure that keys are secured and access is limited to an as-needed basis.

5
Outsourcing Delivery Services

Valerie Horton and Greg Pronevitz

Although in-house delivery is common, particularly among single library systems with multiple branches, the more popular method is to contract out to a commercial carrier. As noted in chapter 1, in a 2008 survey slightly more than half of the respondents reported using commercial services as their delivery source, and another 7 percent used a combination of commercial services and in-house delivery. Add to that the 4 percent who reported using a national shipper like UPS or FedEx, and it is clear that outsourcing delivery to commercial carriers is a common activity for many delivery systems.

According to the Messenger Courier Association of the Americas, there are at least seven thousand courier companies nationwide, ranging from the small "two guys with bikes" messenger services to large, multistate corporations with huge fleets and multimillion dollar budgets. There are significant differences between mom-and-pop messenger services and those larger companies. The messenger services are often located in a single metropolitan area and deliver legal and other documents in a matter of hours. The regional firms, which may cover one state or a dozen, specialize in delivering film, financial records, legal documents, medical supplies, and flowers, to name just a few items.

The complexity of the carrier landscape makes it difficult for courier managers to find the best partner, and, unfortunately, many rural and small communities have no delivery companies. If a delivery business is available in a rural community, as with many small businesses there is a high probability that it will fail over time. Given the difficulty of transferring from one delivery service to another, most libraries would do well to avoid the smaller delivery services. For the purposes of this chapter, we focus on the larger regional carriers that may operate within a significant part of a state, an entire state, or across several state lines.

WHY OUTSOURCE DELIVERY?

Why outsource delivery? is the main question a manager needs to consider. There are significant advantages to running your own courier, primarily the ability to customize your routes and schedules to meet the needs of usually a specific set of libraries. When it is your truck and your drivers, the control remains with the delivery manager. Further, the carrier industry is volatile; delivery companies can go in and out of business at alarming rates.

Outsourcing is attractive to library managers for several reasons. First, economy of scale can save money. If a courier service is already going to every town with a bank and a pharmacy, than adding a stop at a library divides the same cost three ways rather than two. This works particularly well for systems that deliver across a wide geographic region; outsourcing saves on the price per mile driven and on the wear and tear on vehicles. Another reason is that many courier managers do not want to payroll drivers or maintain fleets. There may not be the physical space available, or the ability to repair and service vehicles, or the expertise in-house to know how best to manage such systems. It is not uncommon for those who manage their own fleet to be on the road themselves when a driver is missing from work, and this sacrifice is not desired by many delivery system managers. Further, the library courier manager who outsources does not have to deal with driver payroll or training, liability, or insurance issues.

Perhaps one of the least recognized and yet most important reasons has to do with the difference in knowledge and culture. Employees who drive or repair trucks are very different from employees who work in reference or cataloging. Many library managers have neither experience in the logistics industry nor knowledge about supply chain management. For these managers, devising a route, choosing which trucks to buy, and hiring good drivers and mechanics may seem far too unrelated to a librarian's core job. For many managers, knowing that someone with expertise in these areas is overseeing this part of the delivery operation—namely, their contracted courier company—is a great relief.

TRENDS IN THE CARRIER INDUSTRY

Libraries know very little about the carrier industry. In fact, it sometimes seems that librarians and delivery business people speak different languages. Terms like *break bulk, demurrage, reefer units,* and *zone skip* are not part of a librarian's typical working vocabulary. Given the interdependent relationship between libraries and their contract carriers, the more the two groups know about each other, the better.

This section includes answers to questions library courier managers want to know about the carrier industry. Three people who know the carrier industry agreed to answer ten questions, sharing their insights about the field: Becky Atcheson (formerly national sales manager, RR Donnelley Logistics) has spent twenty years in the courier industry working on a regional and national basis in operations, human resources, as well as sales and marketing. Becky also has ten years of experience in proposing, implementing, and servicing library transportation systems. Ken Bartholomew has more than twenty-five years of leadership experience in executive sales and operations and start-up businesses. Ken is currently president of American Courier, a multistate courier, warehousing, and freight forwarding company. David Millikin held numerous positions at a global industrial packaging company for six years, working in transportation, sales administration, strategic sourcing, and business process improvement areas of the company. For the past year and a half he has been developing new services at OCLC as its product manager for library logistics.

1. **How would you describe the current state of the carrier industry overall? Is it growing, steady-state, shrinking?**

    David: The transportation industry is changing in numerous ways, but costs in the industry are rising as a percentage of gross domestic product (GDP). Total logistics as a percentage of GDP was about 9.9 percent in 2006, according to the Council of Supply Chain Management Professionals, and transportation costs increased by about 9.4 percent in 2006.[1]

    Ken: The answer depends on the type of courier service in which your company specializes. Many courier companies were started to support scheduled route work. Route work means deliveries made on specific times and dates to predefined stops in sequence. A route that goes from library A at 9:00 a.m. to library B at 9:15 is an example. In recent years, route work for both film development and banking records has decreased as their businesses have changed in response to electronic imaging and digital print. As a result, revenues have declined. Other industries supported by courier service have flourished—pharmaceutical, diagnostic, and auto parts to name a few. As with any business, it is important to recognize trends, adjust, and identify new opportunities in other industries that require or will benefit from courier service.

Becky: Historically, many couriers began transporting paper items on an expedited or on-demand basis. Bank check processing, legal documents, and similar items were the basis for much of their route structures. With the use of technology and the Internet, these types of shipments have decreased in volume. Other industries and items have taken up volume in systems, such as pharmaceuticals, lab samples, office supplies, and retail distribution. Although the courier industry specializes in time-sensitive shipments, the size, handling, and volume of shipment have changed. As with any for-profit organization, they must change with market demand.

2. **How do you see the carrier industry's capabilities meeting the specific needs of library delivery?**

Becky: I believe the regional carrier industry is best suited to meet the needs of the library delivery systems because of the flexibility it offers in the overall transportation industry. A regional carrier is a company that services one, several, or twenty states, as compared to a nationwide service like FedEx. A regional carrier has the ability to work with library systems to offer options in service (e.g., same-day, next-day, downstreaming), packaging (e.g., boxes, recycled bags), and labeling (add specific library identification numbers).

Ken: It's a perfect fit. Courier companies are experts in time management and route efficiency. In addition, they provide same-day service and do not have the same strict shipping restrictions of the major national delivery companies. Relieving the expenses incurred and daily management of the library staff is a win-win for both organizations.

David: An academic and business-oriented focus on transportation and logistics is something libraries have not had historically. Libraries are just now realizing the enormous cost potential to be had centralizing logistics services from the thousands of individual branches to larger groups and network-level business organizations. The logistics profession has much to add to streamlining of library operations; and, at the same time, I also believe that libraries have a lot to teach logistics operations in terms of workflow automation and handling data. I see some carrier organizations as better positioned to serve the broad library industry, and some carriers that are more geared toward the local delivery environment, depending on the needs of an organization. Libraries must be careful in choosing partners that will work for the long run and are progressive and financially stable. I see innovation as the key for libraries working with carriers—carriers need to bring new technology and process design to the table if they are going to help libraries save money.

3. With continued fluctuations in fuel prices, how is the carrier industry currently accounting for these costs in its pricing to customers?

Ken: As in the library system, we fine-tune our business as much as possible to absorb cost fluctuations. However, if costs continue to increase beyond reason, we have no choice but to pass them on in the form of rate increases or fuel surcharges.

Becky: In the transportation industry, obviously fuel is a great concern as we attempt to "manage" the cost fluctuations. These cost increases have to be absorbed at some level. A fuel surcharge is imposed on all transportation-related services. When an efficient courier commingles customer shipments, the cost increase should be shared among all customers. When a customer's service level requires more dedicated service, the customer should be responsible for the cost of vehicle fuel utilization for their service, thus a higher fuel surcharge.

David: Since the late 1990s, carriers have implemented fuel surcharge tables that allow them to adjust the prices charged based on the price of fuel. This process gives carriers needed flexibility, because they can neither predict the volatility of fuel prices nor absorb costs that are too high. Carrier company operating margins are too low to have that much flexibility. I see the fuel surcharge as the dominant, most appropriate means for carriers to work with shippers to recover the cost of fuel. Unfortunately, I don't see a way around this model, and it has worked for about ten years now in most transportation companies. I would frankly be wary of accepting a bid from almost any carrier that does not charge a fuel surcharge. It may be possible to negotiate with a carrier to do some hedging—perhaps pay them up front for the maximum volatility expected during the contract period, and then if they don't use the float, they can refund the money. Something like that might work as an alternative, but I seriously doubt this model would gain any acceptance in a fixed-budget, nonprofit industry.

4. **Many libraries have been placed in difficult circumstances when their carriers went out of business. What threats do you see affecting the industry that could cause more carriers to go out of business? What contingency plans should libraries have?**

David: There are several threats in the industry right now:

Driver shortages. This means drivers must be paid more to stay at a company; means recruiting costs are more expensive.

Fuel costs. Volatility means unpredictable expenses for a carrier and can cost carriers millions per year more than budgeted. Also means libraries and other customers have to absorb excess costs.

Insurance costs. Rising insurance costs are always a concern and eat up a sizable portion of a carrier's revenue.

Ken: The courier industry is very fragmented with a low barrier to entry. Shopping rates and committing to the lowest offer can lead to this type of situation for the client. It is important to weigh all factors when choosing a courier. No business is guaranteed to remain healthy, but aiming for a win-win situation with your courier partnership significantly improves your chances for success. It goes without saying that it is cost efficient to avoid interruption of service and loss of time spent securing a new courier partnership. Contingency plans are best addressed during the selection process. Starting off with a credible courier should reduce the likelihood of this happening. Regardless of how thorough your initial review is, you may still find yourself in this situation. I would suggest maintaining a file on all the companies that participated in your request for proposal (RFP) process, in addition to keeping updated route logs from your current courier. Should an emergency arise where you need to replace your courier immediately, you should be able to contact a courier from your RFP list to assist you during your transition period.

Becky: A few issues that threaten the financial stability of carriers in the overall industry could be fuel, insurance premiums, and legal issues surrounding the use of subcontracted drivers versus employee drivers. As libraries assess potential carriers individually, they must perform due diligence in evaluating the financial stability of the company. A financially sound organization should not hesitate to provide a potential customer with financial statements, percentage of revenue of largest customer(s), validation of insurance coverage, and references of present customers. These items should be reviewed on a periodic basis to ensure that the financial stability of the organization has not changed since contract inception. The best contingency plan is to have a "Plan B." Know the other carriers in your area that could perform the services needed. Another viable option is to choose a third party to manage the overall transportation system. A third-party management company oversees and takes responsibility for the carrier(s) performing the service; it has other carrier options within the same market, should the library's carrier go out of business.

5. **How do we know if the vendor is giving us a fair price to our RFPs? What should we look for?**

David: A fair price is most easily confirmed when multiple bids are received from multiple carriers and multiple types of carriers. This ensures that the library has several points of reference to consider when deciding if it is getting a fair price.

Ken: Proceed in this order: call the better business bureau; check several references supplied by courier; visit courier offices in person; speak with a variety of courier staff at each level; and, finally, review and compare prices on the RFP. The RFP should reflect a savings to your own courier operation efforts—in addition to meeting your overall courier needs.

Becky: Understand the costs that are used to determine the final rates presented. Internal costs of transportation management could potentially include wages and benefits, payroll taxes and processing, vehicle costs and maintenance, fuel, vacation and sick time, property/casualty/liability insurance, workers' compensation, supervision/management, facility allocation and other overhead costs (e.g., utilities), and hiring and contracting costs.

6. **Many carriers use subcontracts and independent drivers. What should libraries look for or specify in RFPs and contracts regarding second-party agents? Also, what personnel checks should we require?**

   Becky: Subcontracting is fairly standard in the transportation industry. You should not expect any different service level should a company use independent contractors rather than employee drivers. Background checks with regard to criminal history, driving record, and similar verifications should also remain the same whether the company is subcontracting or using employee drivers. Many carriers use third parties to manage their independent contractors. Determine whether the carrier is using a third party to manage its drivers.

   Ken: Initially, in your RFP, you should ask for respondents to list all subcontractors they will use and to insert language that all future use of subcontractors must be approved by the contracting entity. There should also be language that all subcontractors must maintain the same insurance coverage listed in the contract and that the carrier's use of a subcontractor does not release it from any responsibilities listed in the contract. Most reputable carriers run thorough background checks on their employees and independent contractors, which include motor vehicle records, credit checks, criminal checks, and social security number verification. Drug screening is also becoming common in the industry.

   David: Libraries should just have a strategy—to either accept or not accept subcontractors. If the courier company uses independent drivers, the library should make sure the courier company has a solid process to prequalify such drivers and penalties for bad performance by nonconforming drivers in the contract. Libraries can and should specify anything they feel is important to them, such as driver cleanliness and vehicle cleanliness, when putting together an RFP or contract.

7. **In general, librarians do not understand the logistics business? How can we learn more?**

   Becky: Several organizations offer information regarding the courier industry, including the Express Carriers Association, Messenger Courier Association of the Americas, National Transportation and Logistics Association, and Council of Logistics Management. Many of these organizations have publications.

David: Get involved in professional associations, such as the Council of Supply Chain Management Professionals, Logistics Institute, International Warehouse Logistics Association, Institute of Supply Management, and Warehousing Education and Research Council. Also, it would help to hire graduates with transportation and logistics, operations management, supply chain management, or business process management degrees, or professionals with this background. We need more of these types in the industry to start infusing the broader knowledge into the industry. Get training at one of the many institutions (the most recognized programs historically have been the University of Pennsylvania, Ohio State University, Michigan State University, the University of Wisconsin) that offer basic transportation, logistics, and supply chain management courses.

8. **Some carriers also deliver blood and flowers—a bad mix with books and DVDs. How do we ensure that our materials are protected?**

Ken: All clients a courier does business with should package their shipments to ensure they meet their respective safety measures. Some items must meet strict guidelines imposed by their respective industries or the government. Others must meet stringent shipping procedures or risk product loss—a very costly expense to the client. Professional, well-respected courier companies do not accept deliveries if there is a possibility of contamination. If you have done your research regarding your prospective courier, you will receive premium service.

Becky: All shipments that are transported by a carrier should be packaged properly to ensure the integrity of the shipment until receipt to the end users. It is the shipper's (e.g., library's) responsibility to package shipments properly. In the case of labs items, there are strict requirements from government agencies regarding primary and secondary packaging. If, upon arrival for pickup, the shipments are not packaged properly, the carrier can refuse transport. Accidents do happen, but this should be the exception rather than the rule. When an accident does occur, the importance of insurance coverage comes into review.

9. **How difficult is it to track packages or bins? What kind of costs would that add to systems that are moving five, ten, even fifteen million books a year?**

Ken: Tracking packages ranges from manual application to technology-driven methods. With manual tracking, keeping up with the required documentation can be time consuming and challenging. Scanning deliveries indeed adds costs, but it greatly improves overall communication and tracking of items. The additional costs associated with technology are relative to the overall services and features provided, so they vary. A credible courier should be willing to review a detailed cost-benefit scenario with you.

Becky: With technology today, there is not a difficulty in tracking a package or bin as long as the labeling has some unique identifier or bar code. With library items, the difficulty comes with requests to track individual items within a package or bin. From a carrier standpoint, unless it has been contracted to package individual library items, it should not know the contents of the package. It is up to the library's technology system to track individual items that have been shipped from point of pickup to delivery endpoint. The additional cost for tracking or tracing depends on the technology required, from simple bar code scanning to real-time proof of delivery or signature capture. A good gauge for additional cost would be fifty cents per delivery endpoint for an "average" stop.

10. What are the accepted industry compensation standards for lost or damaged materials?

Ken: We strive never to lose or damage materials. The methods used to ship packages can reduce the opportunity for damage. Closed-lid totes are recommended to minimize damage. Situations do, however, arise from time to time that may lead to such an occurrence. Periodic spikes may occur for one reason or the other, but damaged or lost items should be less than 0.025 percent on average. It is important to have a system in place to establish measurements for condition of items shipped, thus ensuring the condition of each package prior to receipt from the courier.

Becky: The industry standard is $100 per shipment for lost or damaged items. Additional insurance coverage can be made available for extra cost and negotiated at the time of contractual agreement.

By the time this is in print, circumstances related to the carrier industry may have changed. The courier manager must be proactive in finding out what is happening in the field. The Moving Mountains symposiums typically include panels of vendor representatives as well as exhibit tables. Libraries should also consider attending carrier conferences, as listed elsewhere in this chapter.

HOW TO OUTSOURCE YOUR COURIER SERVICE

Once a consortium or library system decides to outsource its delivery service, how does the manager proceed? Self-education is first. A book like this is a great start, but only a start. At a minimum, the manager should contact others involved in delivery to ask questions and learn from their mistakes. There are several ways to find courier managers. A physical delivery electronic discussion group with more than one hundred members can be found on the Moving Mountains website. ALA's Association of Specialized and Cooperative Library Agencies has created a database of consortia: Library Networks, Cooperatives and Consortia. One of the database's searchable fields calls up those consortia that run courier services and includes contact information. By far the best option is to include funds in the start-up budget that allow the manager to visit other regions or states that have an operating courier service and learn firsthand what others are doing with their delivery services.

Finding Vendors

Selecting a vendor is covered in chapter 6. But before you can choose a vendor, you have to find one. This discovery process can be difficult. Searches of better business bureaus and the like often turn up numerous mom-and-pop delivery services that are not appropriate for large-scale library delivery. Managers need to be looking for businesses with millions of dollars in operation costs, not hundreds of thousands.

The Moving Mountain website maintains a list of vendors who have expressed interest in library delivery.[2] But this list is far from comprehensive. Again, checking with consortia in your region is a good way to find reliable vendors. After that, going to the carrier association meetings discussed earlier is the manager's best tactic. The Express Carriers Association has a member directory that gives information on regional carriers. The Messenger Courier Association of the Americas also has a "find a courier" feature. Another newcomer, Courierboard .com, recently launched a site to help find carriers, and it has by far the best interface. Make sure you check as many sources as possible, since they do not necessarily include the same listings.

Planning and Budgeting

The manager must develop a plan detailing the requirements to start up an outsourced courier service. One of the most important elements of a business plan is the budget. Obviously the largest budget item will be the contract with the vendor; information on contracting is found in chapter 6. The following paragraphs discuss items to consider in developing a budget.

The budget must include a salary for a courier manager or assistant. Few if any courier services leave problem resolution and troubleshooting up to the vendor alone. Most outsourced library courier services have a point person who serves as an intermediary between the vendor and participating libraries. Having one person who tracks problem logs, resolves billing questions, and gets to know the delivery company staff is a good way to keep the service on track. Salaries related to managing and maintaining vendor or library relationships are likely to be the second highest cost after the vendor's delivery charges.

Most vendor contracts charge the vendor the cost of providing shipping containers, whether they are bags, bins, totes, or some other container. Shipping containers can be an area of controversy with vendors, especially in delivery services that are growing and constantly need more containers, or where there is a pattern of libraries borrowing the containers for other than delivery purposes. If the shipping containers are not part of either the vendor contract or the participating libraries' obligation, they must be part of the courier service's budget. In 2009, bins were selling for between $12 and $20; shipping bags were less. As services grow, shipping containers can become a significant cost factor.

Although it may seem unnecessary to create marketing materials for a library delivery service, there are good reasons to dedicate part of the budget to marketing. If the manager does not "tell the story" of the courier, someone else will, and that story may not be favorably told. A good way to influence attitudes about a service is to use established sales techniques. One popular marketing item is the van-shaped refrigerator magnet that includes the service's contact phone number and website. Other useful promotional materials include colorful posters that depict the courier service in action and toy vans for the children of the client's employees. The list is endless, and for a small capital investment such items can have a big payoff politically.

Some library delivery systems choose to reimburse for lost materials, knowing full well that the materials will likely be discovered at either the borrowing or lending library. A small pool of money to pay for lost materials can resolve small complaints before they become big problems. It is wise to have clear policies on how the reimbursements are made to eliminate confusion.

Courier management system software is another wise investment. A well-designed management system can assist with participant information, billing records, communication, and trouble log maintenance. At this time there is only one commercial system available, Library2Library from the Quipu Group. Quipu will do a fair amount of customization, which can be very helpful for a courier manager. When preparing a budget, the manager needs to consider both purchasing and ongoing maintenance costs of an information management system. If a system chooses to develop a home-grown system, costs will include technical experts and software development.

Each courier service has unique circumstances that affect its budget. For instance, some services use the USPS or UPS for some deliveries to small libraries. Costs associated with materials, labor, and postage have to be considered. There can also be costs associated with maintaining a courier advisory committee. These costs involve travel or group phone services. Overall, tracking expenses, managing the budget, planning for new expenses, and the like are all important parts of the courier manager's job.

CUSTOMER-VENDOR RELATIONSHIPS

We asked organizations that contract for library delivery services about the status and characteristics of their customer-vendor relationships (or business relationships) as part of the survey described in chapter 2. The survey posed questions to identify the characteristics of good customer-vendor relationships and the methodologies to create them. Responses from forty-three organizations in twenty-one states that reported using a transportation company for delivery services were analyzed. Ten respondents were also interviewed by telephone in a survey follow-up. Ten delivery companies that provide services to library organizations were contacted for further information after the follow-up telephone calls with respondents. Two of these companies responded to our brief questionnaire.

None of these organizations are libraries themselves. Rather, they are consortia, state library agencies, or hosts of shared integrated library systems. We refer to them here as organizations or as respondents. They all contract with a courier for delivery services on behalf of participating libraries. Many couriers also provide contracting organizations with sorting services, such as sorting items at a warehouse for delivery the next day or onboard sorting by drivers. The couriers make most of their stops at libraries, and many comments and suggestions described here refer to libraries. We also cite responses from transportation companies as well as reporting our firsthand knowledge.

The first question we asked was how satisfied the respondent organization was with its customer-vendor relationship. Survey results indicated that 93 percent of respondents were satisfied (49 percent) or very satisfied (44 percent) and 7 percent were unsatisfied.

Characteristics of Delivery Companies of Satisfied Customers

In this section we examine some of the elements of a business relationship, for example, communication, expectations, flexibility, empathy, trust, and contractual aspects. Many satisfied respondents repeated certain themes in describing their couriers. These positive courier characteristics (listed below) correspond to factors (in parentheses) that lead to the successful implementation of a business relationship:

- resolves issues quickly (empathy and flexibility)
- adjusts to meet the needs of most libraries (flexibility)
- uses a single point of contact for library delivery issues (communications)
- understands the organization and libraries (empathy)
- provides quick turnaround time from shipment to delivery (expectations)

Positive characteristics in the area of trust were mentioned less frequently. Only two respondents referred to honesty as a positive factor in their business relationship. Several very satisfied respondents referred positively to a contract. For example, one respondent said, "There are clear, delineated expectations in the contract for both vendor and client. There are measurable outcomes to gauge [whether] standards are being met."

Common Problems

Respondents at all satisfaction levels reported problems with delivery services and with the customer-vendor relationship. The concerns raised most often were about missed stops at a particular library on the scheduled day, off-schedule stops, poor communication about schedule changes, cost, and driver turnover. Respondents also mentioned overloads, where drivers were unable to pick up all the materials at all stops because of insufficient vehicle capacity. These issues may also be categorized into business relationship elements. Missed stops and off-schedule stops often fit into the category of expectations. However, some respondents expressed the need for drivers to understand (or have empathy with) the reasons libraries prefer on-time stops, such as to allow them to schedule part-time or volunteer staff to process materials and avoid having unprocessed materials taking up space in a busy and crowed library. Overloads and driver turnover could be symptoms of financial pressure under which a delivery company cannot afford to provide sufficient vehicle capacity for the workload or afford to increase drivers' payments to reflect fuel cost increases.

Some respondents explained that their contracts do not allow for cost increases when volume or fuel prices rise, possibly fitting into the category of expectations not being accurate at the time of the contract. Recent increases in fuel costs were difficult to predict even two years ago, and systems that implement patron-placed holds for all users or for large groups of new users are very likely to see a significant increase in the volume of deliveries.

Dissatisfaction or a lack of understanding about the cost of delivery services was not uncommon among respondents. It would benefit organizations to learn more about delivery and sorting costs and to have a clear understanding of the current volume and likely changes to volume of items for delivery.

Communications

Communications was a common positive theme in the comments among organizations with a successful relationship. Satisfied and very satisfied respondents cited "regular" meetings and contact with couriers as a feature of their business relationship. Meeting frequency ranged from monthly to annually. One very satisfied organization reported, "I now have quarterly meetings with our vendor. He and I sit down together to make sure everything is on track and to address any issues that either of us sees on the horizon." A single point of contact or a clear hierarchy for different communications for the contracting organization was described as a positive aspect of communications. All follow-up interviewees preferred that the organization, not the transportation company, provide information to libraries.

We received responses from two transportation companies that provided their own perspective on issues surrounding the customer-vendor relationship. We asked how organizations can best contribute to a successful venture. One recommendation was for regularly scheduled meetings. When asked if they had any suggestions to help other organizations that provide courier service to libraries, one respondent responded, "Have one person on the customer side and one person on the vendor side who are responsible for handling all complaints for all libraries. These two people should have a good working relationship."

Drivers' communications and relationships with libraries are an essential part of delivery services. A positive, professional relationship can enhance services.

Respondents described communications between libraries and drivers in both positive and negative terms. The organization's courier manager must exercise professional judgment and ask participating libraries to do the same in order to maintain professional relationships with drivers. Drivers are often independent contractors who are not actually employed by the courier or the organization. Participating libraries should be informed about proper channels for communications to ensure consistency of service.

We asked organizations about factors caused by participating libraries that "soured" the customer-vendor relationship. Some responses indicated that inappropriate library communications with drivers could lead to problems, for example, complaints made directly to the driver or arrangements made directly with the driver for services. Such arrangements can compound problems until they reach a critical point, without the knowledge of the courier manager at the organization or the transportation company management. On the other hand, one respondent felt that the ability to communicate directly with drivers was beneficial.

We wondered if there was any correlation between drivers wearing delivery company identification and contracting organization satisfaction, since uniforms or identification badges are often considered symbols of professionalism. We asked ten follow-up interviewees about driver identification. Our conclusion was that there was no correlation among this group. All unsatisfied respondents reported that drivers wore a uniform or some other form of identification. Among satisfied and very satisfied respondents, three reported that identification was worn, three reported that no identification was worn, and one said, "They are supposed to."

Setting Expectations

Setting expectations is critical to the success of a business relationship. The organization may expect all stops to be made on time, all materials to be sorted and delivered according to a schedule with a certain level of accuracy, all drivers to appear and behave according to standards, periodic reports of delivery activities, and timely, accurate billing. One respondent said that organizations should "express expectations at outset of relationship" to improve a customer-vendor relationship. From the courier side, expectations could include that participating libraries have materials ready for pickup, that they be prepared to take delivery at scheduled times, that the volume of delivery be within certain limits, that new stops be within reasonable driving distance of anticipated routes, and that the courier be paid in a timely manner.

Some problems reported by survey respondents were attributed to the inability of the organization and courier to set expectations accurately. For example, improved technology encouraged requests for materials from more libraries, resulting in a significant increase in the volume of delivery or the number of stops. This caused overloads. The delivery contract was based on a per-stop cost that did not factor in volume of materials. The courier apparently signed a contract without a provision for changes in volume and was attempting to live up to the agreement with limited resources.

Fuel price changes are another important area for setting expectations. Some respondents expressed concern about the rapid rise in fuel prices and how that might either drive prices up or service quality down. Some respondents had contracts that do not allow fuel surcharges. Nevertheless, they seemed to be waiting for the "other shoe to drop."

Flexibility

One transportation company representative's comment directly addressed flexibility: "Be open to change, understand there may be issues that arise which are beyond the vendor's control and keep communications open." Libraries and delivery companies alike are compelled to adjust to many variables such as the weather, traffic conditions, vehicle breakdowns, driver illness or injuries, library workloads, volume of patron requests, holidays, as well as driver turnover, hiring, and training. In follow-up interviews, some respondents expressed a tolerance for the occasional turnover and an understanding that new drivers and sorters face several challenges and need time to get over the learning curve and increase productivity and accuracy. Reports about transportation companies providing services in the face of increasing fuel costs and increasing volume demonstrate vendor flexibility.

Organizations that have experienced serious problems with delivery services can attest to the fact that problems are all relative. What one organization sees as a serious breach is a minor inconvenience to others in a tougher situation. Developing an ongoing relationship with appropriate delivery service representatives allows an organization to use the proper channels to manage problems. Regular meetings at a mutually agreeable frequency can foster constructive communications and eliminate a situation in which problems are the only topic of conversation.

Empathy

Taking each other's perspective is important to a satisfactory business relationship. A lack of understanding of your business partner's situation can lead to unreasonable expectations and misconceptions about the seriousness of problems. An organization's or library's staff may think that it is simple to see things from a "library" point of view, but the carrier's perspective must also be taken into consideration. Several respondents expressed the need for mutual understanding. One satisfied courier manager said, "We understand one another."

One very satisfied courier manager advised, "Work closely with the delivery vendor to help them understand why the libraries act the way they do," and added that it was useful for her to learn about the transportation business because it helps her develop creative solutions. Comments by other respondents expressed the need for libraries to understand that the delivery company is not part of the library world. Business relationships with delivery companies may create a challenge to new courier managers because they are not accustomed to dealing with this new type of contractor. Unlike traditional library vendors, staff and managers at delivery companies are not always familiar with or trained to sell to or provide services to librarians. Often they do not share librarians' language or point of view. In addition, the level of supervision of independently contracted drivers is minimal compared to the level librarians are often accustomed to.

A transportation company representative suggested that "customers . . . be fully informed of standard operating procedures, issues, actions, corrective measures, trends, and new developments." In other words, have empathy with your delivery vendor by doing things in the agreed manner.

Trust

Trust was not a frequently mentioned topic in the survey results. It was mentioned a few times in describing transportation company characteristics, as noted above, and it was implied in the suggestions of three respondents on how to help others develop a good business relationship:

- Write some kind of relationship-building activities into contracts.
- Increase communication from both sides. Consider the vendor part of the team, and keep everyone in the loop.

• Develop a real partnership in which all issues are open—delivery service costs and profits and all of the organization's volume statistics and expectations.

A transportation company representative stated, "Communication and trust are the major tools to maintain a fair and equitable partnership." Conversely, one unsatisfied respondent indicated lack of trust by expressing skepticism that the transportation company would deliver on service promises.

Contracts: It Pays to Put It in Writing

Survey respondents had many suggestions related to contracts. Several respondents focused on the need for a contract. Other respondents suggested that contract terms helped ensure high-quality services and advantageous pricing. We go into considerable detail on the contents and benefits of contracts in chapter 6; here we look at the process from the vendor's point of view.

We asked representatives of delivery companies for suggestions to help library organizations understand more about contracts with transportation companies. One replied, "A contract is a partnership where both parties must benefit in order for everyone to win. If at any point in the contract an issue becomes one-sided, then the contract is not fair and equitable."

During follow-up interviews with targeted respondents, indications arose of possible conflicts or imbalances between contract pricing and costs. When delivery experts discuss costs, it is usually the cost per mile and time on the road that are most significant in a library delivery contract. Some organizations have negotiated agreements that do not include provisions to address increasing fuel costs; others have formulas that predetermine fuel surcharges.

The experience of survey respondents suggests that, when increases in fuel prices are not addressed, the transportation company's reaction might be to limit the size or number of vehicles serving a particular organization. This can lead to one of the commonly listed problems—overloads. Some organizations are compelled by state procurement rules to make contracts that are fixed in this manner. Still, the rapid increase in fuel costs in 2007 and 2008 could not have been predicted, and apparently some transportation companies did not include a high enough price to cover costs and allow for a fair profit. Similarly, a contract that is based on a per-stop price with no factor for increased volume can lead to imbalanced prices and costs that force transportation companies to make decisions that reduce service quality.

It is probably fair to say that it would be useful for organizations and transportation companies to come to a mutual understanding of the risks and rewards for all parties that could result from changes during the term of a delivery agreement: inflation, fuel prices, volume of items shipped, number of stops, distance between stops, and delivery window of time and accessibility at each stop. The focus of such issues and trends in survey responses and comments was mainly on increasing fuel costs and increasing volume of library materials. Both parties should understand that, although not likely, such trends can also be reversed.

It is a challenge for some library organizations to understand transportation companies' business models and their costs of providing services. When responses to an RFP are received, organizations might question whether a higher price equates to improved service, and one respondent said that he felt a transportation company's bid was too low. There are not apples-to-apples comparisons of delivery costs among organizations because of variations in the volume of items shipped, number, frequency, and density of stops, and sortation needs.

We believe it is difficult for an inexperienced transportation company to estimate the costs of providing library delivery services accurately. Bids from different companies can vary significantly, even if they are responding to an RFP to provide the same service that is currently offered with the same routes. The offer to provide the identical service at a drastically reduced price may have little chance for long-term success.

Understanding the bases for costs and prices can help determine measures for improving services that enhance productivity and keep costs reasonable. Knowledge of the cost per mile and per hour for different-sized vehicles and operators may help an organization and transportation company resolve overload problems at a fair price. An understanding of the sorting rate per person may suggest that improved sorting procedures, sorting site setup, and library processing and labeling could benefit parties that use centralized sorting sites. Determining the typical profit margins for delivery companies can provide an understanding of business norms. Such an enhanced understanding could be considered a vast improvement over the situation in which an organization has little or no control over and little basis to predict future costs and prices.

Some respondents expressed a need to contract for a fixed price for a fixed term with little flexibility. Such agreements can lead to higher prices, because the delivery companies are compelled to predict the future cost basis and volume of service and inflate estimates to protect themselves. One transportation company representative said that, in a three-year agreement, he expected to make the most profit in year one because profit would decline in future years due to increased volume of items.

Sorting Practices and Customer Satisfaction

We looked for correlations between the organizations' characteristics and their satisfaction with the customer-vendor relationship. The strongest indicator of satisfaction was the method of sorting. The highest level of satisfaction was found among organizations that used on-route sorting by the driver and for organizations that contracted with a large parcel transportation company that requires individual packaging or labeling for each destination. In these two categories, respondents were all very satisfied. On-route sorting was used exclusively by organizations with the smallest delivery volume (under 100,000 items per year), and the parcel transportation company was used by one organization reporting volume under 100,000 items per year and another reporting volume of about 500,000 items per year. There were also no unsatisfied respondents among organizations for which libraries did the sorting. One respondent was very satisfied and five were satisfied. Of these organizations, only one handled volume exceeding one million items per year.

It was not possible to compare delivery costs across a range of organizations accurately because of variables in the size of the service area, miles driven, volume of items shipped, and frequency of delivery. All these characteristics would affect the size and number of vehicles required as well as the staffing needs for sorting. Nevertheless, we looked at cost factors and customer satisfaction. Respondents reported the total annual cost of delivery service. Figure 5.1 demonstrates that the largest number of respondents had budgets of less than $1 million and similar levels of satisfaction. The single organization with a budget over $1 million responded as very satisfied. One respondent commented that his organization's contract is a large part of the courier's business and that he believes the courier makes efforts to provide responsive customer service and a reasonable price to retain this business.

The survey did not allow us to calculate information to consider the detailed cost of providing delivery services against level of customer satisfaction. We did want to explore the relationship of detailed cost to satisfaction. In follow-up interviews, we determined the average cost per item delivered for ten respondents. The responses indicated that cost per item delivered is not a reliable indicator of satisfaction. The respondents with the highest cost and lowest cost per item

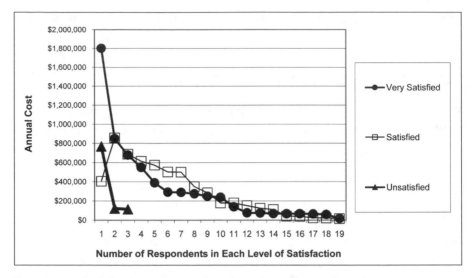

Figure 5.1   Satisfaction measured against annual cost of service

both responded as very satisfied. All three levels of satisfaction overlapped with respect to cost per item delivered for other interviewees.

Lessons

Local preferences and budgets among libraries and organizations that contract for delivery services strongly influence their decision making. For example, one very satisfied respondent had the highest per item cost because its libraries grew accustomed to a particular large parcel transportation company's successful efforts. The libraries served by this company incur higher labor costs to package and label all outgoing materials. Other respondents accept a lower level of service because of affordability. In fact, one unsatisfied respondent described pricing as the best aspect of the customer-vendor relationship. Several respondents described a lack of understanding about what a reasonable price should be; as noted previously, one respondent put the service out for bid but was unsure that paying a higher price would ensure good service.

There is room for further study by contracting organizations on mileage costs, vehicle and operator costs, sortation, warehousing costs, and typical profit margins for transportation companies. Having access to reliable benchmarks will assist them in decision making. These organizations need to begin with a good understanding of the actual volume and traffic between libraries to use this information effectively. Some respondents were not able to describe their volume easily. Others rely on their transportation company for these figures.

Responses indicated that some respondents have a fluctuating perception of their customer-vendor relationship. At times they are satisfied and at other times they are not satisfied. One respondent had a totally different perspective on the customer-vendor relationship in the few weeks that passed between filling out the survey and a follow-up phone call. In this case, the change was for the better.

Changing and conflicting perceptions are not unique to the library community. It is not uncommon in other industries served by transportation companies. John Kerr, contributing editor to *Logistics Management,* wrote this: "Ask most shippers if they're happy with their third-party providers of warehousing or transportation services and their standard answer is 'yes.' Scratch a little deeper, and the real perspectives start to emerge—perspectives quite often summed up in gripes about missed deliveries, missed opportunities, and persistent miscommunication."[3] Kerr went on to cite studies that show that such issues are not totally one-sided. Third-party providers feel that they lack all the necessary information to develop services in the best manner possible.

What do we learn from this? We learn that the customer-vendor relationship is a two-way street. All parties play a role in the success of delivery programs— the transportation company, the organization contracting for services, and the libraries on the delivery routes. If the relationship is professional and consistent, there is an improved opportunity for customer and vendor satisfaction, both of which are necessary for success. There are many elements to a successful business relationship and many challenges to implementing them successfully. However, our survey demonstrates that most of the customer-vendor relationships are successful in terms of customer satisfaction. Striving for the highest levels of satisfaction can lead to improved customer service and, in the end, library patron satisfaction.

VENDOR ABANDONMENT OR DISASTER PLANNING

The carrier industry is volatile—changing as film and banking disappear as business components and most companies scramble to find alternatives. As stated earlier by Ken Bartholomew, the start-up cost to launch a delivery service is low and as a result either the marketplace can have a glut of companies driving down profit margins or the industry can get overheated with mergers, with companies buying each other in cutthroat fashion.

Another problem with the industry is the role of independent drivers. Almost all companies use some mix of in-house employee drivers and independent drivers. These drivers are just that—independent. A 2007 survey by the Messenger Courier Association of the Americas found that drivers are not well paid: 38 percent were earning $7–$10 an hour and only 5 percent were earning more than $20 an hour.[4] Issues with service training, insurance, and liability are constant problems for the industry. Many companies have outsourced the driver contracts to a third party as a way of minimizing the liability problems. This trend can add another layer of problems for the library service.

Further, as mentioned earlier, the price of fuel has been steadily increasing, putting additional pressures on individual companies, as has the price of insurance and liability coverage. When gas hit $4.00 a gallon, profit margins disappeared and business closures became common.

Given this potentially dire situation, what should a library do? Maintaining an in-house fleet and drivers means business will continue, but gas prices and liability insurance and other pressures felt by the carrier industry are also felt by the in-house courier manager. More than one in-house courier manager has spent the day on the road when a driver failed to show up. A manager might consider having more than one carrier service under contract, but the contracting process discussed in the next chapter invariably leads toward multiyear contracts to provide stability of delivery and gain volume discounts.

So what is left to do? Basically, there is only one thing a manager can do in advance, and that is to know which larger couriers do business in the region. Using services like the aforementioned Messenger Courier Association on a regular basis can help a manager stay informed. However, many states, particularly the more rural and western states, may not find regional or statewide competition. For instance, Idaho does not have a statewide carrier as of this writing.

The more knowledge the manager has of the carrier industry, the better. Ways of learning through library channels include attending library distribution and courier industry conferences, asking questions, developing relationships with vendor who you are not contracting with at the time, and reexamining in-house delivery options on a regular basis. All can help you in a disaster situation. Unfortunately, there are no perfect solutions.

A HYBRID IN-HOUSE/OUTSOURCED MODEL

A third model for managing a courier system is a hybrid of the previously discussed in-house and outsourced systems. This is a reasonably common model;

it tends to develop where an existing library system delivery to branch public libraries or between campus libraries expands to delivery to other libraries nearby. Missouri, as an example, runs a fleet of its own trucks to some members and contracts with a courier service for delivery to others.

There are several advantages to this model. A local library system delivery service to branches or campus libraries already has a fair knowledge of what is involved in maintaining a fleet, which can be used to negotiate with carrier companies. The in-house system may want to use a commercial carrier to do long routes to save wear and tear on the in-house fleet or to handle stops that are inefficient to provide in-house because of great distances or low volume. All of these options are worth exploring when you are developing a plan for establishing a courier service.

Notes

1. James A. Cooke, "Logistics Costs under Pressure: 7th Annual State of Logistics Report Finds That Rising Prices and Interest Rates Will Soon Push Logistics Costs above 10 Percent of GDP," *Logistics Management* (July 1, 2006), www .logisticsmgmt.com/article/CA6352889.html.
2. Valerie Horton, "Moving Mountains Project: Physical Delivery of Library Materials" (2008), www.clicweb.org/movingmountains/MovingMountains CourierCompaniesSuppliers.html.
3. John Kerr, "3PL Relationships: More Than a Contract," *Logistics Management* (September 1, 2007), www.logisticsmgmt.com/article/CA6477625.html.
4. Messenger Courier Association of the Americas, "MCAA 2007 Survey Results" (2008), www.mcaa.com/pdf/Survey-Results_2007.pdf.

6
Contractual Vendor Relations

David Millikin and Brenda Bailey-Hainer

Many libraries and consortia have long-established practices to handle their diverse delivery needs. An organization's needs sometimes change, however, or it must reassess those needs in the face of rising costs or other budget constraints. When this happens, the organization must identify new solutions to serve its constituents at lower costs or with better service. During such a situation, the organization should evaluate appropriate alternatives and choose the best new solution based on its latest requirements.

Just as many other library services are selected through a formal bidding process, the best way to identify a delivery service that meets specific needs at the most cost-effective price may be to go through an RFP process. Whether a new delivery service is being established or delivery services are already in place, issuing an RFP can help identify potential new providers, and the process can be leveraged to gain the most advantageous pricing from available providers.

If the organization is not ready to commit to a purchase, other types of documents may be substituted for the formal RFP, including an RFI (request for information) or RFQ (request for quote). These do not usually lead to a binding answer or request process between two parties; rather, their purpose is for a supplier of goods or services to provide information about its offerings. Outside the United States, the RFP may be referred to as an RFT (request for tender).

The RFP process can be daunting. Libraries that are part of city, county, or state government may have to adhere strictly to mandated purchasing practices. The entire bidding process may even be orchestrated by a government employee who specializes in purchasing. In other situations, it may be the responsibility of library or consortium staff to handle the entire process from start to finish. This chapter is designed to provide advice for either situation.

KNOW YOUR BUSINESS

The first step in preparing an RFP is to gather sufficient information about the organization's needs. This means knowing its current shortcomings and strengths and considering what it needs to provide excellent service to participating libraries. Whereas the library community usually refers to *delivery* or *courier* services, in the transportation industry this is usually referred to as *logistics*. Having business knowledge about the organization's logistical needs means knowing several important factors, often called *metrics* or *key performance indicators* (KPIs). Figure 6.1 can be used as a guide for KPIs that should be measured and tracked for the most complete and successful cost-saving or service-enhancing RFP.

COST METRICS	SERVICE METRICS
total spend	number and kinds of materials being transported
cost per unit	transportation modes used
cost per piece	frequency of deliveries
cost per shipment	number of stops or pickups
total accessorial cost	weight and freight class of packages shipped
accessorial cost per shipment	freight lanes and stop locations
cost per mile	contact or address information about each stop
	operating hours
	on-time delivery requirements at each destination
	kind of customer served (e.g., library, office, patron)

Figure 6.1 Logistics metrics

In situations where a delivery service is already being used by the library or consortium and an RFP is being issued to seek competitive pricing, logistics metrics collectively can be used to evaluate the current logistical effectiveness. Depending on the organization's goals—whether more focused on service or cost—some metrics may be more useful than others at determining how well run the logistics operations are. For example, an organization that strives for excellent end-user service and is less budget constrained may have a very high *cost per unit* but with correspondingly high *on-time delivery,* the metric that organization weighs highest in considering carriers. Such an organization should consider ways to reduce *cost per unit* while maintaining or increasing *on-time delivery.* For organizations with tight budget constraints, *cost per unit* and *total spend* are key metrics in determining organizational effectiveness. Therefore, the goal of the RFP process may not be to pick the lowest-cost service provider but to choose the best provider for the organization's specific cost or service goals.

KNOW THE CARRIERS

Logistics companies are critical partners that serve as a link between the shipping facility and the receiving facility. Choosing a weak link for this critical role can lead to lost or damaged goods in transit through theft or rough handling, late deliveries, or even lawsuits in the event of unexpected accidents. Choosing the right carrier can result in a positive experience by the shipper and receiver, low costs, and on-time deliveries.

The library community relies largely on courier delivery service to perform outbound transportation between multiple libraries or to patrons. Courier service is the delivery of small packages and messages, and it is often the most cost-effective service to transport the millions of small packages from libraries. Transportation inbound to libraries is usually via companies that offer less-than-truckload (LTL) transportation, which includes loads with one or more pallets of freight but less than a truckload. Since most inbound LTL shipments are paid for by material suppliers and are not managed by libraries, we do not go into great detail about managing LTL carrier relations or the RFP process for them. Instead, we explore courier service providers as the primary transportation providers to libraries.

There may be opportunities to improve service or reduce transportation costs by managing inbound shipments centrally across a large number of libraries (via a consortium or cooperative arrangement). Carriers may require a minimum level of volume in order to provide a competitive bid. Aggregating many individual libraries or small consortia into a larger regional or statewide group may reduce costs in the long run.

In the United States, libraries generally choose a local or regional courier, the USPS, or one of the large parcel transportation companies—UPS and FedEx. In the transportation industry, these large companies are generally referred to as parcel or package companies—not couriers—although many in the library community call them couriers and they do offer some courier-type services for higher rates. Local or regional couriers often make excellent partners with libraries because they offer same-day local delivery, are willing to transport anything from the size of an envelope to dozens of transport bins, and provide their services at reasonable costs. These companies operate fleets of delivery vans or straight-trucks and usually employ local drivers.

The USPS and large parcel companies all offer courier-like service but, because of their size and complex supply chain systems, are often unable to provide hands-on, customized, same-day delivery like local couriers. On the other hand, their size and coverage enable them to compete with each other in longer-distance, individual package shipments when next-day or longer lead-time delivery is needed.

Whether working with large or small transportation companies, a professional partnership relationship with the company allows an organization to anticipate and understand important changes in the relationship with the carrier. For example, if fuel prices are increasing and cause a carrier to raise its rates, the organization with a good relationship can work through the cost change with the carrier and plan for these changes. If a carrier has a weak relationship with a library or organization, the organization may receive a price increase notification in the mail, followed by a rise in prices a month later, which could have been anticipated and possibly even avoided had some dialogue taken place with the carrier.

Library staff should maintain a professional relationship with carrier representatives at all times. In the past, carriers received more business from their customers by offering personal incentives, such as sports tickets, excessive meals, and gifts, but these practices have generally been unacceptable for years in most industries. Among other things, they distract library workers from focusing on their business objectives in dealing with the carrier—choosing the best-service, lowest-cost provider for the organization.

A library should try to confirm that all carriers under consideration are financially stable and would not have to raise rates in the middle of the contract just to stay in business. Some would argue that the financial stability of a carrier is not the responsibility of a library. But the library is responsible for ensuring the ongoing success of its transportation program and patron satisfaction. Confirming a carrier's financial viability is critical to ensuring the success of the organization's transportation programs.

To determine a carrier's viability, an organization should consider the practices of the carrier to see if it seems to be cutting costs that might affect delivery times or safety. For example, a carrier that does not carry adequate liability insurance because it is trying to keep costs low may be cutting corners elsewhere, such as in routine vehicle inspections and maintenance. Although practices like these may be acceptable for a little while, if the carrier continues them long term it runs the risk of having a serious accident or loss that causes it to go out of business.

Another telling factor in a carrier's behavior is rates that are too low. Low costs are desirable, but if rates are too low for too long they are not sustainable and eventually must be increased to keep a carrier from going out of business. For this reason, when an organization compares rates between multiple carriers, extremely low prices should always be challenged for the benefit of both the carrier and the organization.

Questionable cost-saving practices and excessively low rates are telling factors for a company tottering on the edge, but the surest indication is the carrier's financial statements. Although requests to see statements may offend some companies, carriers that want your business try to communicate openly and will attempt to meet such a request at some level.

Before choosing carriers for an RFP, an organization should find out carriers' capabilities and whether these capabilities are what the organization needs. Finding carriers that fit an organization's needs requires thoughtful investigative questions and open, honest answers from the carriers. Often, organizations contract with carriers that claim to have specific strengths but actually have no experience performing the tasks that would give them strengths in those areas. Contracting organizations find themselves disappointed in these situations and often have to incur the start-up costs required to allow the carriers to learn how to do what they claimed they could do in the first place. To avoid this situation, when investigating potential candidates for an RFP, organizations should ask for references for specific examples of work the carriers have performed to back up their claims of strength in specific areas.

Contracting organizations should also make sure that a carrier's strengths are matched to the organizations' needs. For example, if an organization needs a carrier to stop at multiple branches each day, the carrier should have experience doing multiple stop runs with the drivers it would select for the organization's business. A contracting organization should also make sure that carriers are able to work during the hours of operation required by the library, and that the carriers can meet driver safety and appearance requirements (such as uniforms and grooming). These sometimes minor concerns, if not described as expectations in the initial RFP, can lead to a disruption in the carrier-shipper relationship.

Finally, finding carriers that express their intent to innovate or improve service throughout the contract should be an important goal of the RFP process. Innovative, financially stable carriers are often interested in finding new ways to serve their customers and proactively reduce or maintain costs. Organizations with the most success during this process are those that work with proactive, helpful, financially stable, innovative carriers.

The purpose of the RFP process is to find the transportation company that best suits an organization's business needs. Although close relationships and solid investigation provide confidence that the selected carrier is the right one for the business, finding the best carrier means including at least three carriers in the RFP (if possible) and maintaining leverage in the business transaction throughout the process. Organizations should take care to select several carriers that fit its needs and to let each carrier know that it is not the only organization participating in the bid. With several viable candidates, an organization may even work with each carrier to share the business, and after the bid it can maintain an informal relationship with the losing carriers that may become useful later. This lets all carriers, including the winner, know that they must work hard to get and keep your business.

Creating competition between kinds of carriers is useful as well. For example, a library wishing to bid its business to one of several local couriers should also try to include other regional carriers, some of the big U.S. parcel carriers, or the USPS. Although some of these carriers may not be the final selected option, including multiple carrier types sometimes allows an organization to see other opportunities it may not have seen if bidding only to local carriers. For example, one option may be to bid a portion of the business with specific stops, routes, and times to a local courier and to bid another portion to a parcel carrier based on the number of packages, package dimensions, weights, and destinations. An organization may find through this process that one of the parcel carriers is actually more cost-effective than the courier, or vice versa. If not, the organization can at least plan how much additional cost it may incur in the event of a service failure by the winning carrier.

THE RFP PROCESS

Timetable

When an organization begins the RFP process, it should establish an expected time line for work to be done both inside and outside the organization. Time lines should include the beginning date of the process; the amount of time for the organization to prepare; the number of days or weeks for the participating carriers to prepare; a date for the bid to be sent to the carriers; a response date for carriers; a review date by which the institution commits to participating carriers to have reviewed the RFP responses; a decision date; an estimated time line for the winning carrier(s) to sign the service agreement; and the official start date of the business. Meeting deadlines that are set for the RFP process establishes trust and confidence in both carriers and their contracting organizations, so meeting these deadlines should be a high priority for all parties. When RFPs are handled through a government purchasing office, failure to meet deadlines usually results in the disqualification of bidding companies.

Interaction with Other Organizations

Local, county, or state law may require organizations to follow mandated processes when creating an RFP. These laws may dictate the winning conditions for a bid, RFP time lines, companies that are or are not allowed to participate, and other important factors. Institutions may be allowed to participate in government discounts that have already been negotiated on their behalf. Therefore, institutions should become familiar with such regulations and business situations before starting the RFP process and check for state lists that might indicate contracts already in place that can be used to achieve substantial discounts on services.

For smaller institutions considering the RFP process and for consortium members, in a growing number of areas consortium-run deals may already be in place. It behooves an institution to learn more about these deals before sending out RFPs to potential carriers. It may also make sense to continue the RFP process and compare the results to the expected cost of using a consortium-managed deal.

Creating the RFP

The process of creating an RFP for transportation service can often be laborious and time consuming. It requires a considerable amount of data gathering about one's organization (logistics KPI) and coordination with people who would be considered stakeholders in the deal (e.g., dock workers, sorters, packers, catalogers, administration, patrons, branch staff). To ensure that an organization has a complete understanding of its business, the manager should hold conversations with these stakeholders to understand how the service might affect them. In many cases, stakeholders have a lot to say about the use of potential transportation partners and the details of the services required to meet their needs.

Besides the practical value these discussions have, stakeholders feel like they are part of the process when their input is received and incorporated into the RFP process. Their participation is especially important when the new business is implemented and stakeholders must interact with the service provider. Stakeholders are more likely to cooperate and benefit when they were involved throughout the process of identifying the service provider.

After the initial buy-in from all stakeholders, the RFP document is developed to include all information about the business that the service provider must know to perform its service, including the following elements:

- introduction describing the library or consortium issuing the RFP and reason for the RFP; include links to websites for additional background information
- conditions for participation, such as legal right to transport commercially (federal or state motor carrier authorization); insurance levels; size of fleet; minority ownership; fleet ownership by company, owner-operators, or mixed
- submission procedures including address to which the response should be submitted and number of copies or instructions for electronic submission; RFP time lines with key deliverables and due dates
- contact information of the contracting organization for administration of the RFP and any questions during the RFP process
- scope of work: number of participating institutions; branches; geographic area covered; address and location information of each location served; delivery and pickup requirements and times at each location; number of shipments, pieces, packages, stopoffs, drops, etc.; operating hours; special packaging requirements; any unusual delivery or pickup requirements; security clearance conditions
- daily operational requirements; driver appearance and behavior requirements; vehicle condition
- price expectations or centrally negotiated fuel surcharges required of the carrier

- payment terms, such as who is responsible for paying the bills and what the freight terms are (e.g., who is responsible in the event of loss or damage)
- statement that the RFP responses are binding in the event a carrier wins the bid

Another set of key elements are the expectations the carrier should explain in the RFP. Wording should allow the carrier flexibility in responding to cover the following items fully:

- statement of work: specific lanes (particular routes or modes of transportation materials will travel between specific locations) and stops included in the price; hours of availability; limitations such as maximum package weights or dimensions; dates or times not available (such as holidays); locations that cannot be served
- proof of meeting conditions for participation
- price of the service, broken down to the level at which it is useful for an institution to compare across bidding carriers or versus previous cost levels
- contact information during the term of the contract; business hours and emergency contact information
- background checks: guarantees of driver etiquette and performance; corporate profile describing the company, including physical locations; annual reports, audited balance sheets, or other proof of financial stability; references, including contact information, for a minimum of three current customers

The RFP is meant to establish the conditions and business requirements for carriers to do business with an organization. Some elements may be optional on an RFP but should be discussed and added to the business agreement once the business is awarded.

Carriers may want to negotiate payment terms—such as payment within fifteen days of service or monthly payments. In some cases, carriers may offer a discount for early payment of invoices (e.g., 1 percent net ten days). These terms are usually favorable toward the paying institution. This and other payment arrangements should be worked out based on the needs of the institutions and carriers. Institutions should remember that much of the useful transportation information, such as number of shipments and packages shipped, is recorded on freight bills, so whatever is agreed should be carefully considered by the contracting institution.

In some cases, it may be useful to require the winning carrier to provide monthly or periodic reports on its business performance. Reports from a trusted partner allow an institution to save time recording details about the transportation service performed on its behalf. Reports are also useful when a contract term is about to expire and the contracting institution must gather details about the service requirements for a new RFP. Reports may provide information such as number of shipments, number of pieces and packages transported, actual service times, and other metrics. Before the library manager requires extra work of the carrier to create reports, the manager must be sure to know how the information will be used.

Finally, many carriers have old or outdated "tariffs" that in some regions may be charged in the event that a rate has not been specifically agreed to between the carrier and institution. These tariffs are usually high compared to a negotiated rate and should be specifically excluded if necessary via use of the RFP instructions and the final transportation agreement. A simple clause stating that published tariffs are not applicable in the event that a rate is not available and that all rates must be agreed to in writing prevents hidden charges from appearing on an invoice.

What Not to Put in an RFP

What not to put in an RFP is sometimes as important as what to include. An institution should generally not include things that are transportation industry standard requirements of all companies or things that would be ethically irresponsible. Transportation industry standards that do not need to be included in an RFP include driver's logs for long-distance shipping, safe driver operating hours, compliance with laws, and vehicle safety and conformance with emission regulations. In addition, do not include prices that have already been offered by other carriers or other information that damages the competitive nature of the bidding process.

Reviewing the RFP Responses

A well-written RFP should be understood easily by carriers and will prompt them to respond with an indication that they received the RFP. Carriers ask questions and should be afforded equal opportunities to discuss service options with the contracting organization. Fair and equal treatment of all carriers during the process helps ensure their respect. Common practice for library RFP processes is to have potential bidders submit questions electronically, then all potential bidders are sent copies of the questions and answers to ensure that all bidders have access to the same information.

Once all the questions are answered, carriers should start to submit their responses. As a courtesy when receiving responses electronically, be sure to notify the bidding company that its response has been received. The contracting organization is responsible for reviewing each response carefully. Once all bids are received, the review process should consider each carrier's bid equally. The organization should attempt to clarify anything confusing in any of the carriers' responses rather than ignore such issues.

An astute reviewer of a bid should note any extremely low or high costs quoted by the carrier and, if appropriate, determine whether such quotes were mistakes. Although it may be appropriate to force a carrier to follow the price quoted in such situations, those situations could also cause the carrier to lose money and ultimately have to increase rates. Clarification of such "likely mis-quotes" is appreciated and respected by carriers and also strengthens the relation-ship and trust.

If not prohibited by a formal government RFP process, it is useful to estab-lish a committee to review the responses. This committee should include various stakeholders who will be affected by the decision. This committee can become the foundation for a user committee, since the information gained in the RFP process will be relevant to the development of the service. For example, if the bid is issued by a consortium of libraries, it is good to have representatives from different con-stituencies to be served by the carrier. This might include someone from a library with exceedingly high volume, representatives from both rural and urban areas, and at least one person who works directly in ILL or is responsible for packaging materials for shipment and receiving the inbound shipments. It is useful to cre-ate an evaluation grid that looks at various aspects of the RFP. This grid would include the key questions in the RFP and a place for rating the responses. Such a tool helps quantify the responses, particularly in cases where the amount of information received in the responses is immense and unwieldy.

A reviewer should look at the total cost of each carrier bidding to determine which offers the lowest-cost solution. The specific details of the service should be reviewed for the carriers that offer the most promise, to make sure that the ser-vices offered are what the institution needs. Costs must also be within the scope of the institution's budget and should reflect the services offered.

Overall, once the review process is finished, the reviewer should be satis-fied that he is choosing the best option. In many cases, a selection can be aided by asking carriers to make a presentation on the offered services. Having an operations-level person, such as a dispatcher or billing manager, visit the institution's operations and facility could also ensure that the services offered by the carrier are actually what they will deliver to the institution.

Once a final selection has been made, as a courtesy it is standard practice to notify all respondents that a finalist has been selected and that the organization is entering into contract negotiations with that company. It is a good idea to maintain cordial relationships with the respondents that were not awarded the contract. At some point in the future, if the selected contractor becomes unreliable or goes out of business, one of those other companies may be desperately needed to take over deliveries.

As negotiations with the selected respondent begin, keep in mind that the RFP and response to it should be made part of the legal contract that results. This prevents companies from making claims in their RFP responses that cannot be kept and protects the library or consortium as the contracting agency.

Ultimately, a carefully crafted RFP process that includes a well-written and detailed RFP with sufficient detail about the organization's needs and a sound analysis of the responses should result in a proper match between carrier and library and a solid business relationship that benefits both parties.

NEGOTIATING THE CONTRACT

A contract between a carrier and a library or library organization defines the details, expectations, performance requirements, and everything else about the relationship—including under what circumstances the relationship can be terminated. As with any relationship, boundaries and structure are essential for it to be strong and positive for both parties. The contract is the document that establishes the boundaries of a business relationship. A well-written contract is essential to establish all the necessary elements of a business relationship and to enable parties to interact with clear understanding of all the expectations and consequences for failures.

Contract Rules

The four main elements for a contract to be binding are (a) mutual agreement, (b) consideration, (c) competence of parties, and (d) legality of purpose. *Mutual agreement* means that both parties must have agreed. Either verbal or written agreement is acceptable, depending on the value of the contract and other factors. *Consideration* means that an exchange of things of value occurs in the execution of the contract. *Competence of parties* means that both of the agreeing parties had authority to contract with the other, neither party was under duress to make the agreement, and both parties were in their "right minds" when they made the contract. Finally, *legality of purpose* implies that contracts for illegal purposes are not legally enforceable.

Contracts should be made in writing. According to the Uniform Commercial Code Article 2 (called the Statute of Frauds), verbal contracts are not enforceable for the exchange of goods worth $500 or more, or for a contract that cannot be fully executed within one year, or for real estate contracts, unless evidenced in writing.

In the RFP process, the carrier establishes a binding understanding that it can perform services offered through the RFP at the price quoted. Because a library organization would reasonably make financial planning decisions relying on a carrier's response to an RFP, the services and prices provided in these responses can usually be enforced through legal proceedings if necessary, depending on the nature of the RFP response and process. On the other hand, if a library organization causes a carrier to understand that it is offering business to the carrier through a poorly worded RFP, the carrier could require the library to meet that obligation, including giving business to the carrier. Therefore, a library should not make any verbal or written remarks that could imply that it intends to give the carrier business until the library has actually come to such a decision. One simple way to do this is to inform all carriers on the RFP that multiple companies are being considered and that no offer is implied or intended by the process.

After a library accepts a carrier's bid, depending on the complexity of the business being contemplated, a letter of intent (LOI) may be requested by the carrier or offered by the library organization. An LOI is a formal, sometimes "mini" agreement between two parties that acts as a placeholder until the final agreement and business arrangements can be made to begin the full service. An LOI enables both parties to invest resources toward the full business deal, with consideration (exchange of something valuable) for backing out of the business deal before the business begins. LOIs are most practical when business is complex or takes a long time to begin, but they can also be written to establish trust between two parties where no formal relationship already exists.

After intent has been established, the parties are ready to agree formally to the terms of the business relationship, and they pursue a contract together.

Writing the Contract

Although the contract is the core of the definition of a business relationship, practices in library transportation management vary widely when it comes to the quality, depth, and even in some cases existence of a contract between libraries and their carriers. A well-written contract is critical to establish the boundaries and rules of the relationship.

Most carriers offer a "standard" contract that provides the basic legal requirements of a contract, such as transportation rules and regulations, the carrier's self-imposed liability limits, rates, fuel surcharges, a pointer to the carrier's standard terms and conditions, and extra fees and charges. These contracts may include some valuable aspects that should be in a library organization's final contract with the carrier. In many cases, however, a carrier's standard contract is written more to the benefit of the carrier than to the library and may not meet the needs of the library organization or the specific needs of the business relationship. Therefore, it is important that the organization closely review any standard contract offered.

If feasible, a library organization should prepare its own contract language with the help of legal counsel. The organization should strongly consider engaging a lawyer with expertise in transportation law to request a standard shipper-based (the library is considered a shipper), courier-focused contract template, and to request help in modifying the language to meet the needs of the business. If you are uncertain which law firms offer transportation advice, such expertise may be found at the Transportation Lawyers Association (www.translaw.org).

Common Elements of a Contract

A contract between a library organization and a carrier should contain elements common in most business contracts as well as language specific to the transportation industry. Such elements are often referred to as "boilerplate" language and are common among transportation- and nontransportation-related contracts. Boilerplate language is often overlooked by business managers, but it makes an important difference when issues arise from the execution of the business arrangement.

The following elements should be included as boilerplate language in transportation contracts, and like any part of the contract these sections may be negotiated to the satisfaction of both parties:

Definitions. In many contracts where industry-specific language is used, parties should include definitions at the beginning of a contract to define such language for the benefit of the parties and mediators or judges in the event of a contract dispute.

Address and legal name. Contracts should always specify at least one full, legal address of all contracting parties. Without addresses, it may be possible for a party to dispute that it was the party of record on the contract. For example, a company named "ABC Courier Services" may exist in more than one city.

Choice of jurisdiction. To make litigation easier on one of the parties, parties may agree to the laws of a certain state or local jurisdiction. For example, parties may agree to submit to the laws of the state of Ohio, if the library organization is headquartered in Ohio. This clause may cause hardship or difficulty for the defending party if that party does not have offices in the agreed-upon jurisdiction because it forces that party to travel to defend or pursue litigation.

Choice of forum. In the event of a contractual dispute, parties can agree to other forms of mediation, such as binding mediation by a judge outside a courtroom. This clause can be useful to reduce the cost of legal expenses in the event that litigation is needed. However, if it is agreed that settlements will be decided outside the court system, a mediator's judgment is legally binding on both parties, and neither party can go through an appeals process if the mediator's decision is not satisfactory.

Term and option to extend. Contracts should have a beginning date and an end date, which define the *term* of the agreement. Parties may, however, agree to an ongoing relationship, the term of which is to be reviewed periodically. This kind of agreement, which may never end according to its own language, is often referred to as an *evergreen* contract. For contracts that have a definite end date, but for which parties wish to extend, they may include an extension clause to indicate the conditions for extending the agreement.

Attorney's fees. In the absence of an attorney's fees clause, parties in litigation are usually responsible for paying for their own legal expenses. Parties may, however, agree that the losing party must pay all legal expenses.

Indemnity. The indemnity clause is typically included in a contract to ensure that the carrier protects the library organization against the carrier's negligent or willful errors in running its business, where such errors or negligence cause loss, injury, damage, or loss of life to a third party to the agreement. For example, if a driver employed by the carrier kills a person while transporting a library's materials between branches, such a clause would ensure that the carrier must defend the library from any lawsuits that the family of the deceased may bring against the library.

Nonperformance penalties. Well-written contracts must include language that provides explanations of what *nonperformance* means and what happens when a party breaches the contract through intentional or negligent nonperformance. For example, libraries should consider the consequences of situations such as the courier failing to pick up or deliver a shipment on time; a driver acting inappropriately; an invoice being charged incorrectly; or a carrier failing to hold adequate insurance through the life of the contract. Without clearly defined consequences, it may be difficult for a party damaged through nonperformance to rectify the situation with the other party, or even for a court to assess damages in the event of a loss. Consequences should always match the severity of the damage caused. For example, a library organization may experience a loss of service to its patrons by a late delivery; it should determine what this is worth, or how the carrier can make up for such an incident.

Inclusion of other agreements. If other agreements exist between the parties (written or verbal), the parties may agree that the current agreement constitutes the entire agreement of the parties and no other agreements are implicitly or explicitly included as part of the current agreement. Or, parties may agree to incorporate terms of other agreements in the current contract by referring to them in the current contract. Usually, if other contracts exist, the parties agree that in the event of a conflict between the contracts the terms in the current contract supersede previous contract language.

Assignment. Although unlikely, a library organization may allow the transportation company to pass the responsibilities of a contract on to another company to perform the duties of the contract. Passing an agreement to another company is called *assignment.* In most cases, after all the work an organization does to pick the best carrier for its business, it wants the contract to be performed only by the carrier originally contracted. Organizations should include a clause that the contract may not be assigned to any other party except by written agreement.

Independent contractor. The contract should specify that it does not create or imply a partnership between library organization and transport company or make the transport company an agent or employee of the library organization. Without this clause, it may be possible for the carrier to claim that it has an employee-employer relationship with the library organization, which implies greater responsibility and liability on the part of the library organization. This provides protection in addition to the indemnity clause, specifying that the carrier is responsible for its own actions and that the library has no control or direction over the carrier's decisions made to perform its business.

Severability and survivability. A court may find one or more parts of the contract not enforceable due to a conflict with laws. In such a situation, a library organization should protect the rest of the agreement and business relationship with a severability clause. This allows portions of the contract to be severed from the agreement while the remainder of the contract is still enforceable. In addition, parties may wish to make parts of the agreement binding after the term of the agreement ends. This situation may arise with regard to unresolved damages between parties or when certain paperwork should be kept for legal purposes after the contract term.

Anti-waiver. If a portion of the contract has been breached and has gone unenforced for a time, and new behavior has been established by the parties, then the damaged party that has accepted the new behavior cannot force the other party to rectify the damage. If, for example, a library consistently pays late for services, and the carrier has not charged late fees, the carrier cannot suddenly change its behavior and charge late fees for previous payments or force the library to start paying late fees, because a new contract or behavior has been implied by the actions of the parties. An anti-waiver clause is provided in contracts to prevent the past behavior of parties from overriding the contract. With an anti-waiver clause, in the case of late payment by a library, the carrier could start charging late fees to the library even if such charges have not previously been enforced.

Written modification. After the contract has been signed, verbal modifications to the agreement may be made and enforced, unless a section in the contract limits modifications to be acceptable only through a written modification. Specifying that modifications to the contract must be in writing ensures that no confusion exists between the parties about the terms of the agreement.

Notices. Usually, courts do not recognize verbal or copied notices as binding to the parties of a written agreement. Parties may, however, agree in their contract that changes or notices may be accepted via facsimile or electronically to make communication easier between the parties.

Time is of the essence. Time may not be a business-critical factor in the performance of a contract. In other words, if a supplier makes goods and ships them to a buyer a few days after the planned delivery date, if the buyer is not held up by such a delay, no damages would result from the delay. But in the business of transporting goods a delay may result in a patron using an alternative information source, such as a commercial book dealer or information provider. To some libraries, this may or may not mean a loss of business. Therefore, it may make sense for some organizations to state that "time is of the essence" in the performance of the contract to recover losses due to the delay.

Force majeure. Force majeure is a contract section that states that neither party is responsible for loss or nonperformance resulting from events outside the reasonable control of either party. Such events are frequently referred to as "acts of God," such as war, catastrophic weather, or a worker strike.

Captions. Captions are usually present in well-written contracts to help a reader more easily identify sections of a contract. However, if not otherwise specified, a caption may be interpreted to change the meaning of a contract. Therefore, it is appropriate for a clause to state that captions are included for the benefit of legibility and are not intended to affect the meaning of the contract.

Transportation-Specific Contract Language

All elements of the preceding list are common in contracts related to transportation and other business relationships. Because transportation of goods has historically been heavily regulated, additional language should be added to contracts that relate to the transportation laws. This section focuses on the legal issues pertaining to transportation.

Bill of Lading

A bill of lading (also called a *waybill*) is a legal document that describes the contents and date of a shipment and may include writing that describes terms and conditions of acceptance of a delivery. Either carriers or library organizations may supply the bill of lading. Usually, the receiver of a shipment must sign the bill of lading to indicate that the items delivered are in good condition, that no pieces are missing, the date received, and that the carrier is released from any further liability from the shipment. The terms of a bill of lading are legally binding when the receiver signs for a delivery, even if the library organization has not read the terms on it. In some cases, though, writing on the bill of lading may conflict with the terms of the contract, in which case it is important to include language in the contract that specifies that the terms of the contract supersede those on the bill of lading.

Insurance Limits

Requiring insurance in a contract ensures two things for the library: that, if faced with the expenses of a serious accident or a high-dollar lawsuit, the carrier will be able to continue its services without going bankrupt due to these expenses; and that, if a lawsuit is brought against the carrier, the carrier has enough insurance to cover the expenses of a lawsuit against it and can help prevent the library organization from being sued by the injured party. Transportation contracts should include a section that states how much insurance the carrier must carry in the areas of general liability, cargo liability per incident and per year, and umbrella insurance. Contracts should also require carriers to hold the state minimum requirement for worker's compensation insurance. An institution should require carriers to list the institution as additionally insured, to ensure that a loss against the institution is paid directly from the insurance company to the institution.

General liability insurance protects against claims from a wide variety of factors, such as general operations, sale of goods, and ownership of property. In transportation, general liability insurance is especially important in covering expenses caused by major accidents and injuries. A practical rule is to make sure that, if the contracted carrier is sued for a serious accident, the liability coverage is enough to cover a reasonable claim against the carrier. If the carrier lacks adequate liability insurance, liability for such a major incident could fall on the contracting library organization in a lawsuit. Insurance is, however, generally meant to manage risk and cannot foresee all frivolous lawsuits. An institution should not require a carrier to overinsure itself or it may risk increased prices or a carrier that can no longer afford to do business with the institution.

Because of the potential for loss or damage, contracts should require carriers to hold cargo insurance for the maximum reasonable value of shipments.

Umbrella insurance is like "last resort" insurance, useful in the unfortunate event that a carrier has multiple large insurance claims in a year and its general liability coverage is expended. Most carriers do not have to tap into their umbrella insurance, but those that do can sometimes prevent bankruptcy by having the additional insurance at their disposal. If a library organization is contracting with a carrier to haul very large volumes of freight and is therefore exposed to a high risk of damage or losses that can occur on the road, it may be in the library's interest to require a certain amount of umbrella liability coverage.

Transportation Rates and Accessorials

One of the most critical components of a transportation contract is the definition of costs for services and the methods of modifying those costs. Before writing the prices to be paid in the contract, institutions should learn what rate structures and price increase processes their carriers follow. For example, some carriers wish to review pricing every year; others may wish to have flexibility in pricing if serious market fluctuations affect their operations. It is appropriate for a carrier to request, and for a library to agree to, a method for a carrier to modify prices over the course of a long-term contract. It is also usually appropriate for an institution to require price changes in writing, so that verbal quotes over the phone are not considered final until both parties sign.

Institutions and carriers also should agree on the terms of payment. Commonly, carriers accept fifteen- or thirty-day payment terms; some offer a 1 percent or other discount if payment is received within ten days. In addition to the payment terms, institutions should agree with carriers on the consequences of late payment, including how many days past due is considered late payment. Institutions should make sure that their accounts payable processes are prepared to make payments as arranged in the contract to make sure late charges do not unexpectedly increase the costs of the service.

Although the primary charges for a carrier's work can be described in a schedule of rates, many costs are unpredictable or are charged based on specific work performed by a driver. For example, some carriers charge a fee for helping unload a vehicle or having to unload a delivery in a difficult pickup place. Another performance-based expense is fuel cost. As unpredictable as fuel costs are, carriers cannot adequately recover these costs in their base rates. Therefore, most transport companies now charge a fuel surcharge in addition to their standard rates. Fuel surcharges are usually based on a national, regional, or locally published index that states the average fuel price for the previous week or other period of time. They also assume that a carrier has calculated in its rates some base level of fuel expenses, so that the surcharge recovers only the excess amount of cost not included in base rates.

All of these extra charges are called *accessorial* charges and may be negotiated with the carrier when setting the contract. Accessorial charges are usually written as addenda to a contract. Addenda can be useful to set off components of an agreement that may change from time to time. If standard shipping rates are expected to change over the course of the contract, it may be appropriate to reflect these in an addendum to the contract as well.

Subcontracting Organizations

Transportation companies come in two primary organizational structures: those that are asset owning (have trucks, drivers, and other transportation equipment), and those that work without transportation assets. Those without assets broker work between a shipper and a carrier or a group of carriers to perform the work required. Brokers are not usually directly liable for the work performed by an asset-owning subcontractor; asset-owning carriers are directly liable for the work performed with their own assets.

Transportation laws define the relationships among brokers, carriers, and shippers in the event that contracts do not spell out a broker relationship. If a carrier under contract by a broker causes injury to the library or a third party, the broker may be liable for the injury due to the broker relationship with the carrier. In many cases, though, the nature of the relationship between a broker and library organization must be clearly spelled out in a contract, so that the library is protected in the event of nonperformance by its broker's carriers.

When contracting with brokers, library organizations should make sure that the broker will contract with its carriers for all the substantial work and responsibility that carriers would hold if the library organization contracted directly with them. For example, if a library wants its carriers to have $1 million in liability insurance but is working with a broker, the library should contractually obligate the broker to make its carriers hold at least $1 million in liability insurance. If a library wants drivers to wear a specific uniform and be without facial tattoos, the library should contract with its broker to ensure that the broker's carriers comply with this requirement.

Part Three

Managing Physical Delivery Services

7

Routing and Materials Management Systems

Bruce Smith and Valerie Horton

The success of routing materials through delivery whittles down to one word: cooperation. The best-designed material routing systems are those that promote accuracy, speed, safety, and efficiency for both the libraries using the delivery service and the delivery service itself. This can be done only through the cooperative efforts of the delivery service and its participating libraries.

Library material routing through delivery is best studied as part of a complex supply chain. The simple way to view the resource-sharing supply chain is to break it down to its primary purpose, which is to take an item from the shelf of an owning library and send it to another library for patron use, and later to return the item to its shelf location at the owning library. As those who work with delivery know, the journey of an item from shelf to shelf and back is made up of many small steps.

Many variables influence the effectiveness of routing and materials management systems, including

- integrated library system (ILS) or ILL system functionalities
- facility space and design in terms of delivery materials processing areas and delivery exchange access

- whether the delivery service is provided in-house or is contracted with a private courier
- whether an item is being shipped within a library system or consortium or outside it
- whether the item is being shipped to the delivery system's participants or to others
- staffing

There are four main components to a materials routing management system: labeling, sorting, packaging, and handling. In this chapter we relate the basic components of delivery material routing to the path an item takes through the resource-sharing supply chain and how the different variables can affect routing effectiveness.

LABELING

How materials are labeled can be one of the most contentious debates during design of a routing management system, especially when materials are shipped outside a system managed in-house. Each library group within a delivery network has particular processes and ILS- or ILL-generated slips that it wants to use for delivery labeling to streamline its processing of materials. The bottom line is that a labeling system must work for the delivery provider to ensure speed and accuracy according to its internal routing and sorting structure.

It is important that libraries sending materials adhere to standardized labeling and codes as developed cooperatively between the libraries and the delivery service. All information that is asked to be provided on an approved label must be included on the routing slip to facilitate its proper and timely delivery. Because materials may be shipped along multiple hubs when in transit through a delivery system, all hub locations must be indicated on a routing slip along with the final delivery destination.

Other information that is helpful and important to successful material routing is the shipping date and sending location, which are used to track routing problems. If an item is not labeled as it should be, knowing who sent it allows the delivery system to follow up with the sender to correct how the organization labels in the future. Having the shipping date allows participants of a delivery network to know the transit times for items coming from different locations. Should a library see that items take longer to arrive from a particular location than is expected, it can ask the delivery service to work on improving the transit time.

Labels can either be handwritten or generated by the ILS/ILL system. Handwritten labels often lead to routing errors because of improper coding, not enough information, or poor handwriting. Handwritten labels also add a step to the process of preparing materials for delivery. The preference is that routing slips be electronically generated and printed. Printed labels are faster to create and tend to be more accurate and easier to read.

In most ILL transactions, paperwork must be included with the item as it travels between a lender and a borrower for the item to be processed properly. With system-printed slips, it is possible to include the delivery routing information on this same slip. With a handwritten slip, the additional steps involved include having to refer to a delivery network listing to determine exactly how the routing slip should be filled out and then actually filling out the slip as neatly as possible. One pitfall on handwritten slips is that many communities can have several different libraries all using the community name. For example, in a city called Jefferson there could be a public library, a college, and a school district all receiving delivery. It is easy for a sender to just write Jefferson, which results in confused sorters handling the item in transit.

In a closed-loop delivery system, where the libraries receiving delivery are a part of the same system and have delivery service from one provider, it is possible to simplify labeling. In these systems labeling is generally needed only to ship hold or reserve material. Any items that are being returned to an owning location can be sorted according to item ownership labeling. To facilitate speed, it is best that any ownership tags on an item be placed on the front outside cover and conform to the coding system used by the delivery service.

How routing slips are labeled or coded is an important part of a successful material routing system. There are three main ways to do this: having the names of receiving locations and hubs fully written out, using alpha codes that correspond to these names, and using a numeric coding system.

Fully writing out the receiving location names and hubs is self-explanatory. The benefit of spelled-out names over alpha coding is that shortened alpha codes can result in misreading. The disadvantages of full names, mainly with handwritten labels, is the additional time consumed to prepare items for delivery and the possibility of important information being left off the routing slip.

The best alpha codes are created in relation to the receiving location's name. For example, a city named Monroe could be MON. Alpha codes with no relation to the receiving locations names increase the difficulty of sorting and slow down sorting. An example is the OCLC codes, which for sorters are difficult to memorize and often require use of code guide sheets. Alpha coding is easier to memorize than numeric coding but can lead to misreading when codes are similar, like MCF and MFC or FIT and PIT.

Delivery managers constantly strive to decrease missorting and miscoding problems, for both are expensive in terms of staff time and shipping costs. A missort doubles the number of times an item is shipped. Standardizing a shorter, more memorable code can reduce costly mistakes. Both Massachusetts and Colorado report that shifting to a numeric code from a longer alpha coding system has reduced internal mistakes in both systems. Another significant advantage to moving to a short numeric code system is that it makes the automation of management functions through a courier management system easier (see chapter 10 for details of courier management systems). Another key reason to recode a library system is to improve sorting. Anything that improves efficiency in systems sorting millions of items a year has a direct cost advantage.

The process of converting from any library addressing system to another is politically charged. Many library employees have memorized the codes of frequent exchange partners or have preprinted labels and other addressing information. Resistance to change is a common experience for most library managers, and any change process must be managed with care.

Experience from those who have changed their coding system suggests that one of the most important considerations is giving participants plenty of lead time to prepare for the change. One system announced its upcoming change six months in advance of the cutover date. Frequent announcements were made at library meetings and through paper and electronic communication. After the cutover day, the system continued to honor old codes for another six months. On the last day six months after the cutover, any item using the old code was shipped back to the sending library for relabeling, forcing a final conversion to the new system.

Reports from those who have switched to numeric codes suggest that initial criticism is louder and than post-implementation complaints. For instance, Colorado did face some harsh criticisms when presenting the proposed change to participating libraries, but there we no complaints reported about the new coding system in several follow-up surveys. In fact, the loudest complainers had become the best supporters of the coding change. Overall, once the code change was completed, both Colorado and Massachusetts reported that their systems were working better and with fewer complaints and mistaken deliveries.

SORTING

Material can be sorted at the point of packing, on the fly in delivery vehicles, at regional sorting hubs, or at a centralized location. Each method has advantages and disadvantages and works best in different delivery circumstances.

Library presort is always an advantage, for it allows full totes or pouches to move between libraries without further sorting or processing. Drivers simply pick up the full tote and deliver it unopened at the destination library. Unfortunately, many libraries are unwilling to spend the extra time or do not have the space to allow for presorts.

Sorting in driver vehicles can be managed only on routes that move few items, usually in rural areas. Usually the driver's vehicle has a dozen bins labeled with the next libraries on the route. The driver picks up a handful of items at the first library on the route and places those items into the bins for the proceeding stops along his route. The items picked up later on the route for the earlier libraries are left for sorting at a centralized hub. It can be quite efficient to have drivers sort en route but does not work for larger delivery services.

Sorting at regional hubs is efficient but requires duplicate labor and space to manage multiple sorts. If the regional sort does not produce a full tote or pouch, then items are often sorted twice in the process, leading to delivery delays. For larger systems moving millions of items, a centralized sort is usually the best solution.

Sorting materials at a centralized location requires a high level of detail management. There are two main ways to handle a centralized sorting process—manually or with automation—and the management and planning required for the two are quite different. The main difference is in the labeling and handling at the library end of the distribution chain. We first look at what is required to develop and manage an effective and efficient manual sorting operation, then detail the planning and management of an automated sorting solution.

Centralized Manual Sorting

Manual sorting requires coordination between libraries and the delivery service, accomplished by standardizing the labeling practices, tracking delivery volume by delivery locations, and planning centralized sorting workflow to coordinate route return times with the sorter staffing.

Like many processes in the library material resource-sharing supply chain, the effectiveness of centralized manual sorting is measured by the rate at which items can be sorted. The rate of items sorted depends on the amount of handling required to sort the item to its library destination accurately and the amount of distance a sorter needs to walk to move between sort locations. Fewer handlings and shorter walking distances lead to a higher sort rate. Determining and monitoring this rate allows the delivery manager to evaluate the efficiency of the centralized sorting process.

How materials are separated when shipped to and from libraries greatly affects the speed with which they can be sorted manually at a central site. To provide an example of how to determine sorting rates and how to improve these rates, we use the following parameters: materials are shipped in plastic totes that hold an average of thirty-five items each, there are twenty libraries served by the delivery service that send on average one hundred totes of materials to the central sorting location each day, and libraries do not perform any preseparation of the materials.

To determine how quickly sorting staff are able to process materials in this setup, divide the number of totes sorted in a single hour by the number of staff who sorted during that full hour. To get the most accurate rate, perform this sample study a few times over a few different days. In this example, we stipulate that the average number of totes sorted by a single person in a one-hour period averages ten totes, or 350 items. Thus, to sort through the hundred totes of materials received on average each day at the central sort location, ten hours of labor time are required.

Keeping a regular record of how many totes are picked up at each delivery location each day allows you to find out if the sorting rate can be improved. In this example, the library system delivers to twenty libraries. Five of those libraries are part of the city's branch delivery system. This city has the largest population in the library system, and the delivery data indicate that fifty of the totes shipped by delivery each day go to these five library locations.

As noted above, distance and handling directly relate to labor time with sorting. In this centralized sorting setup, the materials are sorted directly into the totes. The totes are arranged on shelves in a square with five library sort locations on each row of the four shelving sections in the square. With the data indicating that half of the materials sorted go to the five locations of the city library, it may make sense to ask participating libraries to place materials destined for one of the five city locations in one tote and items for the other fifteen locations in the other tote. A simple separation like this should not add significant time on the library end of preparing materials for delivery, since the library already sends more than one tote each day in delivery and this level of separation will be easy for library staff to perform.

With this separation, the central sort site can be configured to have the five largest locations on one row of shelves and the other fifteen libraries set up for sorting on the other three rows of shelving. With this new layout and sorting design, a new time study can be done to determine the sorting rate for materials to the five largest library sort locations and the rate for sorting to the remaining fifteen library sort locations. A sorting rate increase would be the result of reducing the distance sorting staff walk when sorting items between the various library sort locations.

Suppose that in our example the rate for the five largest libraries shelving row increased to eighteen totes sorted per labor hour and in the other three rows with the remaining fifteen library sort locations the rate increased to fourteen totes per hour. To get the total number of sorting hours it should now on average take to process the day's workload of one hundred totes, we have $50 \div 18$, for a total of about 2.75 hours, and $50 \div 14$, for a total of about 3.5 hours. Thus the total time to sort through the daily volume has been reduced from 10 to 6.25 hours. This amounts to more than nine hundred hours of labor saved over the course of one year, all made possible with a simple change in the process with a negligible impact on the libraries doing the material separation.

Another way to look at making a separation feasible in terms of impact on the library of is to study the totes being sent to libraries alphabetically. You may find that half of the volume sorted at the central sort site goes to libraries that alphabetically fall between A and M and the other half is shipped to libraries falling between N and Z. This would be another easy separation for libraries to do with little impact on library staffing time. The same concept can be applied to library systems using a numerical labeling code system.

The previous example illustrates how libraries can assist sorting efficiency at a centralized sorting location. Now consider how a central sort site can separate materials being delivered to libraries to improve their handling efficiency at delivery.

Libraries, especially larger libraries, often process incoming delivery materials in different locations in the library according to where particular items need to end up. The most basic separation, and typically most feasible at a central sort site, is that between materials filling hold requests and materials being returned to the library for reshelving. In many libraries, hold materials for patron pickup are checked in at the circulation desk. Materials being returned to an owning library to be shelved are often handled in a back workroom, where they can be checked in and then presorted onto book trucks for shelving.

If all these materials are delivered to a library mixed together in totes, library staff have to go through the extra handling step of separating items for either the circulation desk or the back room book trucks for shelving. This separation could instead be done at the centralized sorting location. The sorting area layout could be designed to have two totes tiered on the shelving, with one tote for "return" materials and the other for "hold" materials. Just as the separation done by libraries is simplified so as to not affect library staff time, this level of separation of materials going to libraries should not have a negative impact on the central sort site's sorting rates.

Such a separation is usually feasible only in a single-hub closed-loop library system. There, it is possible to distinguish between "return" and "hold" simply by giving materials for holds a special label. Items being returned to an owning library could be sorted by ownership tags permanently placed on the items. Sorting staff could be trained to sort materials without labels into the "return" tote and items with labels into the "hold" tote.

In a delivery network where materials are transferred between multiple sorting/delivery hubs, labels are typically required on all items in order to facilitate quick and accurate sorting. Expecting sorting staff at each sorting hub to memorize which libraries are served by which hub in the delivery network is not realistic. This is especially the case when a private courier service is handling the sorting and the delivery, since this courier is likely not as familiar with the delivery network as a library-run delivery service.

Automated Materials Handling

Automated materials handling (AMH) has been in widespread use throughout many industries and businesses in the private sector for many years. In the past ten years, AMH systems have increasingly made their way into the library, particularly in Europe. The majority of these systems have been employed in automating the handling of materials being returned to libraries. A well-designed system can greatly reduce the amount of labor time associated with checking in returned materials and getting the materials back to their shelf locations.

In the past handful of years, AMH systems have been designed for implementation at centralized sorting facilities. More and more companies specializing in AMH have directed their services to this market. The systems currently on the market for centralized library delivery sorting vary greatly in design and potential for return on investment. Determining whether an AMH system is right for your delivery service sorting involves research and several decisions. The purchase cost of these systems, even the smallest, can be quite high. A basic sorting belt system without supplementary container handling conveyance equipment or transport bins can cost at a minimum $500,000. Larger systems with advanced container handling equipment or transport bins can cost $2 million or more. Though an AMII system works for sorting operations of all sizes, budget realities make AMII implementation a possibility only at larger library systems handling a high volume of materials.

Basic AMH functions are really quite simple and generally fall into one of two categories: conveyance of containers and automated sorting. Sorting sites considering AMH are usually most interested in the sorting functions.

In the first category, robotic crane or cart systems have been designed to convey totes at the central sort site. Some of these systems move incoming totes to the sorting system location in the facility to eliminate any manual lifting of the totes. This same system then takes totes that have been filled in the sorting process away from the sorting system location, organizes them according to routes, and delivers them to a loading dock area ready for truck loading and delivery. FKI Logistex designed and installed such a system at the King County (Washington) Library System. This system was designed to work with the plastic totes the libraries were already using for delivery.

In another type of a material transport system, materials are sorted into carts or wheeled bins that also serve as the containers used to take the materials to and from libraries. Seattle Public Library's main library uses such a system, designed and installed by Tech Logic. Materials in the sorting system are placed into what Tech Logic calls Smart Bins, which, after they have been filled, are then simply rolled onto trucks with liftgates for delivery to libraries. Both systems, and those available from other vendors, are designed to ease the physical transfer of materials within a central sort site and on delivery routes.

The sorting system itself, which redistributes incoming materials at the central sort site to their respective library destinations, is typically a belt-driven system with the ability to read bar codes or radio-frequency identification (RFID) tags, communicate with the ILS shared catalog automation software, and place items in a particular library's tote or bin ready for transport. The first part of this system is the induction point, where materials to be sorted are placed into the system, typically onto a conveyor belt. This can be done either manually or by specialized induction equipment.

Once an item is on the conveyor belt, its bar code or RFID tag is scanned by a reader. The reader then connects to the automated catalog to determine where to ship the item. After this information is received by the sorting system, the item travels along the conveyor belt until it reaches the designated library's chute. The belt system is often set up with what is called a cross-belt, which grabs the item and sends it through a chute into a tote or bin for the library. The system can be programmed to have items sorted a number of ways. Many sorting systems are programmed to have two chute locations for each library, so that hold items go into one chute and returns into the other.

There are many factors to consider in designing an AMH system for centralized library delivery sorting:

- whether the system will handle bar codes, RFID, or both
- how materials are inducted into the sort system
- what kind of container materials are placed into as they are sorted
- the facility space footprint required to house the system
- the communication between the system and the ILS automation
- throughput—the number of items the system can sort per hour
- system maintenance
- labor time and costs required to operate and manage the system

The design, functionalities, and costs of AMH systems vary greatly. The best way to investigate the suitability of an AMH system for your centralized sorting operation is to contact vendors, who can provide customer references and work with you to design a system specific to your needs and budget.

Bar Code and RFID

The complexity and potential of an AMH system have much to do with whether library materials are tagged with bar codes or RFID. If the library materials already have RFID tags, then choosing an AMH system with an RFID reader is an easy decision. Having a system that functions with RFID saves material induction point labor time, simplifies the physical functionality requirements of the system, and increases the throughput rate of the AMH system. An AMH system that must manage materials with bar codes can slow down the throughput rate, increase the labor time necessary to induce items onto the sorting belt, and increase the required complexity of the system's physical design. It might, then, seem that purchasing an AMH system that functions with RFID would be the prudent decision. However, since most libraries currently have bar codes on their materials, tagging library materials with RFID is an additional major cost consideration.

The operational functionality of bar codes requires that they be visible and correctly orientated for the bar code reader to scan the item. This requires that items be inducted, or place, into the AMH sorting system in a manner that makes this possible. This can involve manually placing an item with the bar code facing up on a sorting belt or designing the functionality into the AMH for the item to be manipulated by the system to rotate the item until the bar code can be accurately scanned.

Placing items manually into the sorting system has a long-term negative cost impact. The labor time in performing this function is an ongoing cost that grows over time as wages and volume increase. The system must be designed with the capability for having manual induction points along the sorting belt added in the future to increase the number of operators who can feed materials into the system in order to process the delivery material volume in a similar time frame. Without additional induction points, the workday has to be extended to handle any increase in volume. The number of potential induction points is limited by the system's throughput capabilities. This is true for manual or automated induction.

Designing the AMH to orient bar codes for scanning does slow down the throughput, but it allows the system to include automated induction, which in the long run eliminates the labor costs incurred with manual induction.

Advantages, Disadvantages, and Costs of AMH

The decision to convert a centralized sorting operation to AMH usually comes down to cost. As delivery volume continues to grow, managers of sorting operations are constantly trying to find ways to improve productivity and reduce costs. There are often ways that libraries and central sort sites can work together to increase efficiency, but even with exceptional cooperation there is a limit to how fast materials can be handled manually while maintaining accuracy and safety. Realistically, in a manual sorting setup the ceiling of productivity lies in the range of 500–700 items per labor hour. Also, because we are human we make errors, and the faster we try to go the more errors we make. With all this in mind, how do we determine when it makes sense to consider automating the sorting part of the resource-sharing supply chain?

Let's first determine the potential return on investment (ROI) of converting to AMH. Each situation is different, and acting as if you have determined a cost certainty is a large operational leap. Suppose you determine that you can staff an AMH system with two operators. If you are wrong and end up needing three operators, your ongoing labor costs increase by 50 percent, which will greatly affect your return. Still, with such potential uncertainty there are some assumptions and calculations that can provide accurate estimates.

For this purpose we use the following data: the current sorting operation processes 20,000 items on average each day, and staff is individually able to sort 500 items per hour. With these assumptions, 40 hours of staff time are needed each day to process incoming materials. This rate serves as the basis for determining any labor ROI with a move to AMH.

To determine an equivalent rate with AMH, two pieces of information are needed—system throughput and staff time. Assume that the system can sort 2,000 items per hour, which in this situation means that it must operate 10 hours per day to process the 20,000 items currently handled. If only two people are needed to operate the system during these 10 hours, then this operation potentially cuts its sorting labor costs on an ongoing basis by 50 percent. If this operation is run five days per week, 100 hours of labor are saved each week. Over the course of the year, say the hourly wage with taxes is $12.50, or $65,000 saved per year in labor. If the purchase price of the AMH system is $600,000, that amounts to a little more than nine years for the investment to pay for itself.

There are, however, other cost implications. But before we detail them, let us emphasize this important point. An ROI calculation is done with the manager's best estimates and information from the vendor, but there is potential for over-estimating. How do you know if what you think is needed to operate the system is correct, and how do you know if you are getting the most realistic numbers from the vendor? The most important part of the process of researching an AMH system is talking with people from library systems using the AMH system you are investigating. You may hear that this particular AMH system's throughput is actually closer to 1,500 items per hour, or that they found three and sometimes four operators are needed to manage the system. Purchasing and converting to an AMH system is definitely a buyer-beware situation.

So, what are other factors to consider when calculating ROI? First, ongoing maintenance and service are cost items. Most vendors offer yearly tiered service plans to help fit your particular system and budget capabilities. On the savings side, there is a potential for a big advantage by moving to an AMH system, though it is hard to calculate: the potential savings possible at the library end of the supply chain. A great advantage of AMH is that for the most part library materials do not need to be labeled. In our example, if the central sort site is handling 20,000 items each day, that means the libraries are cumulatively receiving 20,000 items each day and preparing another 20,000 items for the next day's delivery. If half of those items need labeling to indicate they are holds going to another library, there are 20,000 items either being labeled or having labels removed each day. If it takes only fives seconds to handle the labeling at the libraries, that could still eliminate almost 28 hours of label handling each day at the libraries served by delivery.

The AMH can be set up to enable bulk check-in of materials delivered in totes or bins, which provides significant staff savings. The system is able to track the specific materials it sorts to a library container. The tote or bin can be tagged with either a bar code or RFID. When the tote or bin is full, it is scanned to correlate those materials in it with the specific container. When the container is received by a library, staff can simply scan the tote bar code or RFID to check in all the materials it contains. This can be a huge staff labor reduction for systems where libraries have to check in materials individually.

Another advantage in many AMH systems is a sorting error rate of only one in 10,000 items. Additionally, AMH systems can trap holds while items are in transit, and sorting and delivery statistics are electronically captured in real time. On the down side, AMH system breakdowns lead to volume backup similar to that on holidays or route cancellations; this causes problems on the days after the closure because the AMH throughput rate cannot be increased.

All these cost and savings factors must be considered when looking at an AMH system. The best way to get the most accurate ROI is to perform time studies of all the handling processes currently taking place at both the libraries and the central sorting facility to determine which manual operations could be replaced by AMH and what efficiencies would be gained. Also, talk with people from a library system using an AMH system about processing rates you can expect. If possible, visit a library system using an AMH system before purchasing; it will be well worth the time and travel costs.

MATERIAL HANDLING CONTAINERS AND EQUIPMENT

In systems that do not have AMH, there are several ways materials can be packaged and moved between locations. Material handling for delivery encompasses two main areas: how materials are packaged, and what equipment or mechanisms are used to move the materials between locations. For those who use a package delivery option such as USPS, UPS, or FedEx, packaging requirements are typically strictly defined. Those systems that use a regional delivery service, whether contracted or in-house, are usually able to work with the delivery service to choose a packaging option that is convenient, easy to use, and affordable for both the library and the delivery service.

As mentioned earlier, a package delivery service has the great benefit of having individual packages closely tracked throughout the delivery supply chain. However, not only does this level of tracking typically come at a higher cost, but the staff time expended packaging and labeling individual packages also adds a high cost to each item shipped. A great benefit of using a regional courier service is the ability to bulk-ship items in a container or bag. It takes far less time to affix a routing label to an individual item and place it in a container or bag than to pack an item in a jiffy bag and label it with a destination's full address.

Canvas Bags or Plastic Containers

Of the many different packaging options out there, the most commonly used by libraries are canvas bags and plastic containers. These are the standards not only in libraries but in most supply chain operations shipping multiple smaller items.

Canvas bags are durable, relatively inexpensive, and can be stored without taking up much space. The bags are often waterproofed, and many have flaps that can be either snapped or zippered shut to contain and protect the materials within the bag. The main disadvantages of canvas bags are that items must be packed in a specific manner to make the bag sturdy for transport, and the bags often must be hand-carried between delivery vehicles and libraries. Both can result in extra labor time. It is possible to stack these bags on platform trucks or two-wheeled hand trucks if they are properly packed, but because they are made of a soft material they are prone to tipping and falling off, resulting in damage to the materials. Also, because these bags do not stack easily, drivers often resort to hand-carrying, which increases the risk of lifting-related injury.

Plastic containers are an increasingly common alternative to canvas bags, especially in systems where delivery volume is increasing. Plastic containers are the standard in supply chain operations in the private sector for transporting library-like materials. Plastic containers—also referred to as totes, bins, or baskets—are extremely durable, often lasting for decades. The most typical used by libraries can be stacked or nested together when empty, so they can be stored without taking up much space. A disadvantage of plastic containers is that the durable ones are also the most expensive. Though it is possible to find plastic containers for $5 or less, these are usually prone to cracking. More durable containers can be found either direct from manufacturers or through material handling supply distributors. A high-quality tote can cost $12–$15 and more if ownership information or logos are stamped into it.

The main benefits of these containers are that they are easy to pack without having to adjust materials to get just the right fit, and they are often designed to interlock when stacked on each other, which allows them to be moved easily on typical platform carts and hand trucks.

Carts and Hand Trucks

Once a packaging choice has been made, the next decision is about equipment for moving the bags or containers safely and efficiently. Two main materials handling equipment options are standard in delivery systems: platform cart and two-wheeled hand truck.

The platform cart is typically designed with a flat deck to place containers on. The deck is set on four casters, two fixed and two that swivel. This cart is best used inside a delivery facility or library to move containers. Because the platform is flat and does not have lipped edges to secure containers from sliding off, this cart is not suitable in outside environments where it needs to be moved over uneven paved surfaces. It is possible to secure containers onto such carts with strapping, but this adds time to the packing process. If containers are secured to the cart, it is also possible to transport them on delivery vehicles outfitted with liftgates.

The two-wheeled hand truck is most frequently used when making deliveries. Containers can be stacked onto these hand trucks for wheeling in and out of delivery locations. There are convertible hand trucks that can operate as two-wheeled hand trucks or fold out into four-wheeled carts. This versatility is useful with routes that can vary greatly in volume.

Another cart option, called the Tote Master, is manufactured by Cart-Tech LLC (www.cart-techsolutions.com; this cart was designed and is being sold in partnership with a material handling equipment manufacturer by author Bruce Smith). The Tote Master is designed to work as a container moving system. It holds two stacks of containers in place on the cart by lipped tabs manufactured into the base of the cart. It is a four-wheeled cart with two fixed casters and two swivel casters and a removable handle for space-saving storage. To use the cart as a point-to-point delivery system, a vehicle with a liftgate is needed.

The system works like this: When totes are packed at a central sorting facility, they are placed on a Tote Master. The cart, with the totes on it, is then rolled into a vehicle's cargo box either at a loading dock or using a liftgate. When delivering at a library location, the driver simply lowers the loaded cart from the truck using a liftgate and rolls the loaded cart into the library location. As outgoing materials at the library are prepared for delivery, they are placed into totes onto carts stored at the library. When a driver brings in the incoming cart, she takes the outgoing back to the truck and, ultimately, back to the central sorting facility without ever having lifted a tote during the entire route. By having the totes on carts at the libraries, library staff are also able to move them around in the library without lifting containers. The idea is to eliminate lifting along the delivery route so larger trucks can be used to their maximum capacity. This capacity reduces the need to split routes to handle growing volume, saving the additional mileage and driver times.

8
Growth Management Solutions

Valerie Horton, Ivan Gaetz, and Bruce Smith

Physical delivery managers are constantly looking for ways of reducing delivery volume. Every time an item is shipped, there is a small chance that it will be damaged or lost in transit. Further, the more items being shipped, the greater chance of ergonomic injuries to staff who pick up, unpack, or carry items. As more items are moved, large vehicles are needed, more drivers, more fuel and tires, and so forth. But the most important reason to reduce delivery volume is that every item shipped has a cost. Particularly for large public library systems that are moving millions of items a year, controlling delivery cost is crucial.

In this chapter we look at five methods of reducing growth and better managing collections: floating collections, which reduce shipment between branch libraries; hold/reserve queue list clustering; reduced transportation holds; cooperative collection development that matches material placement to patron demand; and downloadable multimedia, print-on-demand, digitization, and other electronic delivery methods.

FLOATING COLLECTIONS

As branch library circulations in public libraries have soared, librarians have found methods of reducing the movement of items between branches. In a floating collection, items do not have a permanent shelf location in any given library; instead, they move between system branch libraries. The concept replaces the model of separate library collections held by different branches with one in which a single unified collection floats among various holding facilities. Most items remain in whichever library they are returned to, and it takes a hold request for the item to shift location.

The concept of floating collections has been in practice for decades but has been gaining popularity as circulation numbers skyrocket. Reducing delivery costs is a major advantage of floating collections. Library systems such as Hennepin County in Minnesota and Jefferson County in Colorado have reported significant reductions in moving items between branches, as much as 67 percent and 75 percent, respectively.[1]

Floating collections focus on the patron, since items move to locations where there is demand for them and collections are constantly refreshed. This method also cuts down on material handling, helping to extend the life of circulating items while reducing ergonomic injuries related to shipping. Since items are not shipped back to an owning library, they end up back on the shelf faster.

Most major ILS vendors, such as SirsiDynix and Innovative Interfaces, have floating collection functionality built into their circulation systems. These systems allow for easy reassignment of the physical location for each item. If there is a hold on the item, it is redirected to a specific library for checkout; otherwise it is simply shelved at the receiving library.

HOLD/RESERVE QUEUE LIST CLUSTERING

The terminology of this material routing function differs from one ILS vendor to the next, but the concept and desired results are similar for the goal of improving material handling management efficiency. For example, in SirsiDynix products the function is referred to as *hold clustering;* in Innovative Interfaces, *priority paging.* For the purpose to this section, we use the term *clustering.*

The benefits of cluster groups within an ILS are twofold. They enable the system to fill a hold request for a particular title by retrieving an available item from the best possible location for shipment to the requester's library, and they reduce overall handling of an item placed into the resource-sharing supply chain and decrease the number of individual item sorts at a centralized sorting location.

When creating a hold queue list sequence from a shared automated catalog, the ILS first searches for an available copy of a title at the patron's chosen pickup location. As we all know, if there were always enough available copies of the titles at each library in a shared automated catalog, there would be no transportation issue. Because this is not the case, creating cluster groups as the next search priority in a hold queue list sequence is a valuable tool that can improve delivery efficiency. After searching for an available copy at the requester's pickup library, instead of the ILS next searching for an available copy in the entire shared catalog, it searches a cluster of selected libraries in the shared catalog.

One way to cluster libraries is by grouping those libraries served on the same delivery route. This has the effect of routing materials from the best possible location in terms of distance and transit time. When processing holds for transit, libraries within a cluster are able to either sort materials into "destination" totes labeled to go directly to one of the other libraries their location is clustered with or set aside items in a tote for the driver to sort in the delivery truck that can be delivered en route. The result is that more holds placed in the system are delivered to libraries along delivery routes on the same day they are picked up. Simply put, the items travel fewer miles and are delivered to the patron quicker. An added benefit is that labor can be reduced at a centralized sorting location, since fewer items need to be handled individually by sorting staff.

A drawback to clustering is that, when designed according to routes, the hold demand for items requested by other libraries in a cluster may be too great for a small library within the cluster; this is especially true in systems or consortia with libraries that vary in size greatly. To balance the hold requests fairly within a shared automated catalog, clusters may need to be formed outside existing route structures. Though this means that not as many items will be delivered en route on the same day, transit holds going to other libraries within a cluster can still be placed into destination totes or bags, thus reducing handling and labor costs at a centralized sorting location.

Creating clusters within a hold queue list sequence can greatly improve material routing efficiency. As with other aspects of courier management, this must be done in partnership with libraries in order to achieve a fair load balance of the transit holds filled among the libraries within a shared catalog and according to each library's capacity to perform additional levels of outgoing delivery material sorting.

REDUCED TRANSPORTATION HOLDS

The reduced transportation hold (RTH) is a method for better managing high-demand titles in the hold queue. One example of RTH is available as a module in the Dynix Classic ILS. It allows an item to be trapped at a library to fill a hold for a patron that is not currently first in line in the hold queue for a particular title. The effects of RTH are reduced delivery volume, less material handling and processing time by library staff, and often improved patron fulfillment.

The use of the RTH module by the LINK automated shared catalog consortium in the South Central (Wisconsin) Library System has been especially effective during the initial release of high-demand popular titles. This is exemplified with a snapshot of how holds were filled for the final installment of the Harry Potter series within the LINK consortium's shared catalog. The following is an excerpt from the consortium's newsletter:

> **Reduced Transportation Holds at Its Best**
>
> The 2007 release of *Harry Potter and the Deathly Hallows* provided us with an example of how well Reduced Transportation Holds (RTH) can work for all LINK libraries. Many libraries checked in their copies on Saturday, July 21. On Monday, July 23 we ran some reports to analyze how well RTH is doing. There were 118 copies of *Deathly Hallows* checked out on Saturday and all were checked out at the owning library. As of Monday there were 83 items on the hold shelf and only 2 were at non-owning libraries. There were 20 items in transit to fill holds at other libraries, but 13 of these were SCIDS (South Central in Demand materials purchased by the library system to make extra copies available in the catalog of titles that are in particularly high demand) and it is the job of SCIDS to fill holds at any library. So, of the 221 items that were available for checkout on Saturday, 13 were SCIDS, 199 stayed in the owning library and 9 went out to fill holds at non-owning libraries. RTH kept a potential of 199 items from going into delivery and, more importantly, kept 199 library copies in the owning library to fill holds for local patrons. If we were not using RTH, we would not have had any control of where the individual items were going.[2]

Of course, there are patrons that track their hold list closely and may notice that at times they do not move up the queue for a particular title like they thought they would. In particular a smaller library's patrons in a shared catalog consortium may experience their holds not being filled, though they may be at or near the top of a queue, because the title keeps getting trapped at larger libraries.

However, there are many times these patrons will benefit from this by receiving an item faster than they would have without RTH.

COLLABORATIVE COLLECTION DEVELOPMENT

"Moving mountains" figuratively and aptly describes the work of resource sharing and its physical delivery systems. Mountains of materials are transported, and mountains of obstacles are reduced in the exercise of collaborative collection development. In fact, resource sharing and collaborative collection development constitute a partnership essential to the development and provision of basic library services and resources, namely, the creation of high-quality collections and the needed, effective access to those collections. To be clear about the terms, *collaborative collection development* means collection building in which selection decisions, covering monographs and serials in both print and electronic formats, are made with some degree of consultation among different libraries, and *resource sharing* generally refers to the document delivery of returnables.[3]

There are a great number of collection development arrangements and plans. A shared approval plan for monographs is one well-documented form.[4] Another, quite uncommon as it turns out, is a shared purchase plan. In discussing the partnership between collection development and resource sharing, our main reference is to a particular shared purchase plan, although the insights offered here should relate to most other types of collaborative collection development and their reliance on effective resource sharing.[5] Simply put, the success of collaborative collection development of whatever type largely rises or falls on the depth and vibrancy of the systems and services of resource sharing. By the same token, resource sharing becomes a more vitally important service where the materials shared are of an especially needed, desired, and elevated quality. One cannot function well without the other functioning well.

Since 2005, the Colorado Alliance of Research Libraries has seen an increasing need to conduct collection development in dramatically new ways. This realization brought about the creation of a shared purchase plan that aimed to increase the quality of the Alliance collections as a whole by avoiding needless duplication. The plan was also designed to free up time for bibliographers to concentrate on more specialized purchase decisions rather than those the libraries would clearly need and want. This new initiative in collection development became possible because of several factors, chief among them an efficient and effective system of resource sharing.

Resource Sharing: The Essential Element

In whatever ways collaborative collection development may be expressed and managed, the key element is resource sharing. A basic rationale for this type of collaboration is the ability of participating libraries to make available in an effective and timely manner the materials needed by users. If borrowers cannot readily and easily obtain the materials residing at another library, the pressure mounts for individual libraries, on their own, to purchase all needed items. Library users, especially teaching faculty at academic institutions, tend to argue that materials are needed on-site and that ILL presents a significant barrier to obtaining library materials. Advocates of collaborative collection development counter that certain titles should not be purchased because at least one partner library has committed to obtain those titles and they can be quickly and conveniently accessed by any user. If this turns out not to be the case, if we cannot rely on a robust library courier service, this basic rationale rapidly falls apart. In effect, then, a well-managed resource-sharing system permits libraries to develop and engage collaborative collection development plans in new and dramatic ways.

An important benefit of the resource-sharing collection development partnership is the deeper and broader collection such collaboration envisions. What we cannot achieve individually in terms of a rich monograph collection we can achieve collectively. For instance, Regis University is committed to collecting widely in the specialized areas of Catholic studies and Christian theology at the undergraduate level. This allows Regis partner libraries to collect little in this area and to concentrate rather on other subject areas, such as Buddhist studies and titles in world religions at the University of Colorado and publications in Jewish studies at the University of Denver. Moreover, other partner libraries can scale back substantially in collecting in religion itself and concentrate their acquisitions budgets in other fields more germane to the institution, such as agriculture or hydrology at Colorado State University. It really is rather simple: one library can rely consciously and deliberately on others for materials in low demand locally in order to create enriched collections with more specialized materials of higher interest and probably use. Higher use of materials from the home library holds down delivery costs. It also requires a different way of thinking about collection development. We need to think in terms of the whole collection and not solely the parts. There is no doubt that resource sharing with adequate physical delivery makes this possible and feasible.

The effective resource-sharing system enjoyed in Colorado and Wyoming led the Colorado Alliance to strengthen its internal professional relationships. In particular, its shared-purchase plan required development of more intentional and sophisticated professional relationships among selectors at the partner libraries. This entailed bringing bibliographers together in workshops and conferences to build understanding and trust among a group of professionals who normally would not have much contact with each other, at least contact for the specific purpose of collection development.

Again, it is the resource-sharing system that allowed development of the Alliance purchase plan and new partnerships at the professional level. With these stronger professional relationships now in place, there could be other opportunities for interlibrary collaboration, such as an expert referral network, enhanced interlibrary advise on digitization projects, or collaboration on additional print and electronic journal collections, to name a few.

The resource sharing that makes possible the Alliance plan also serves as an insurance policy, of sorts, for libraries that may face challenging financial times. One objective of the plan is to maintain access to resources appropriate for institutions of higher learning when acquisitions dollars do not keep pace with inflationary costs or when budgetary reductions are mandated. To be sure, however, the plan does not mean that a library can slash acquisitions budgets and expect its partners to cover this deficiency on a sustained basis. This is not the point. In an occasional lean year or two, however, the partner libraries can help an institution still meet its obligations to support and not jeopardize high-quality education or ultimately cause institutional accreditation to be threatened. The plan allows for libraries to pull back when required by the parent institution and to reassign acquisitions budgets where they are most needed. Again, in an important way, resource sharing makes this possible.

Fostering the Partnership

Because of the strong increase in number of published print materials and the generally modest increases or atrophied acquisitions budgets in academic and other types of libraries, individual libraries are increasingly falling behind in their mission to provide needed materials to users.[6] To offset this trend, libraries need to rely more widely and more intensely on each other for interlibrary resource sharing. How can libraries foster this important partnership?

In the first place, now more than ever, selectors and collection managers need to understand and appreciate the work of staff engaged in the various facets of resource sharing. Problems sometimes arise because of differences in "standing" between collection managers who are usually "terminal degree" professionals and resource-sharing personnel who are often at a paraprofessional staff or assistant level. Some professionals tend to denigrate the work of nonprofessionals, and as a result staff persons tend to feel devalued and unappreciated. That is not to deny that sometimes staff persons can be oversensitive about not being at a professional level and can read negatively too much into their interactions with professionals. That being said, where professional snobbery does exist, librarians need to be corrected of the vestiges of arrogance and be led to regard all library workers as team members. Library deans and directors need to ensure that all persons are appreciated for their contributions to the mission and operations of the library, and they should encourage understanding, respect, and appreciation of all employees on an equitable basis.

Good communication between persons involved in resource sharing and collection development would help all involved to acknowledge, understand, and appreciate this partnership. Why not on a regular basis (and it would not have to be that frequent) conduct information sessions for these two groups together? Resource-sharing personnel could discuss the issues and challenges of physical delivery, and collection managers could discuss new directions in collection development. Concrete examples could be shared. Articles on resource sharing and collection development could be circulated among these groups to promote mutual understanding and appreciation. Why not share statistical reports to better profile the workloads of each group? This could help each employee know the challenges and see more clearly what is accomplished by others in these departments. And it is always helpful for supervisors of each department to meet regularly to discuss matters related to both resource sharing and collection development.

Library directors, deans, and other library leaders should take the lead in fostering such a partnership. This could take the form of recognizing the nature of the interdependence of resource sharing and collection development, perhaps by way of written reports, oral communications, formally and informally, within the library. Professional development dollars could be designated to fund courses and other continuing education opportunities for personnel in resource sharing and in collection development. Encouraging employees to participate in regional collaborative collection development initiatives, of course, is a tangible expression of how a library understands and values resource sharing. New technologies (e.g., collection analysis tools that incorporate usage data, systems that notify borrowers and track materials in better ways) that increase efficiencies in both resource sharing and collection development could be purchased. Directors should ensure that the workspace for resource-sharing operations is in no way a barrier to high-level functionality and that it is located as much as is feasible in a setting due the importance of this service. And, most important, as resource sharing increases in volume and complexity, it is important that staffing levels be enhanced appropriately. Undoubtedly there are many other ways to nurture this partnership.

THE IMPACT OF ELECTRONIC DELIVERY

Both physical and electronic deliveries to patrons are important parts of library resource sharing. Electronic delivery is the method of exchanging information electronically through online networks. The more library items move electronically the better, for it helps to preserve collections and reduce transportation costs. The electronic shipment of journal articles and short documents is a well-established practice, particularly in academic libraries. Many types of electronic deliveries are starting to have an impact on physical delivery, including downloadable multimedia, electronic journals, e-books, digitization, and print-on-demand. Many of these services are still in their infancy, but as they grow they have the potential to reduce library delivery volume significantly.

Downloadable Multimedia: Music, Recorded Books, and Film

As Bob Dylan sang, "The Times They Are a-Changin'," and nowhere faster than in the world of downloadable multimedia. Huge numbers of music, film, and spoken-word titles are now available to be downloaded onto personal computers, TVs, portable players, iPods and other MP3 players, and cell phones as well as many other types of devices. As of 2008, commercial companies such as Audible advertise fifty thousand spoken-book titles available, Netflix has twelve thousand downloadable films, and Apple's iTunes has eight million songs available for download by customers. Overdrive advertises that 8,500 public libraries subscribe to their collection of downloadable music, books, and video from their 100,000-title Digital Library Reserve. Overdrive's collection alone is larger than most public library branches.

All of these numbers are from a relatively new industry; the title counts will only grow more impressive over time. If multimedia titles are all available to be downloaded, what kind of in-house collections will libraries have? With the library role as provider for the have-nots, perhaps media collections will continue for some time, but are they likely to grow given the growth of downloadable content? Right now, about a third of materials transported physically are books on

CD, music CDs, and DVDs. We suggest that, even at this early stage, multimedia delivery is probably at or just past its peak and is likely to decrease substantially over time, and probably decreasing in delivery volume substantially over a short period of time.

Electronic Journals

Sharing journal articles has a much longer history than downloadable multimedia in libraries. Unlike downloadable multimedia, which is mostly a public library service, journal use is primarily an academic issue. In 2006, 3,617 academic libraries borrowed 4,615,685 nonreturnable ILL items from other libraries and purchased another 4,093,133 nonreturnable items from document delivery services.[7] Beyond OCLC's well-established ILL system, numerous library consortia are dedicated to journal sharing, among them Rapid, the Boston Library Consortium, and SUNY Express. Commercial providers such as British Library Document Supply Centre, ProQuest's Dialog, and Infotrieve have long been providing articles for a cost. Software systems allow digitized articles to be delivered directly to a faculty or college student's desktop. Within the past few years, large aggregator databases have made finding full-text articles easy and quick for patrons. Companies such as EBSCO, ProQuest, and H. W. Wilson provide numerous databases with millions of full-text articles. Prior to the 1980s, articles and short documents would have been shipped by USPS, at a substantial cost and slow response time. Now, journal articles have almost no impact on physical delivery, except for the occasional shipment of a bound journal, and that is unlikely to change in the near future.

E-books

The electronic book, or e-book, is a newer and less-used format in libraries than electronic journal articles. An e-book is a reproduction of a print book in digital format. In a few cases, e-books have been created that were never intended for print. Stephen King's novella *Riding the Bullet* is a much discussed early foray into online-only publishing. A more common approach is for a print title to be offered in both print and online, or if the item is a reference title to switch from print to online-only availability. Reference materials have made a particularly successful transition to electronic distribution. Most reference titles provide their contents in sections or chunks, which allows for easy online retrieval when searched.

The full text of new print books is also increasingly found in electronic format. Starting in 1971, Project Gutenberg has built toward its current collection of 25,000 free, public domain titles. Most of these books were created by volunteers who typed in the content of classic works from such authors as Twain, Austen, and Shakespeare. Originally, an e-book from Project Gutenberg could be downloaded onto a disc or computer. It could then be read on the computer screen or printed out.

Another early e-book provider, NetLibrary (now a division OCLC), focused on selling content to libraries. With over 170,000 titles, NetLibrary has one of the largest collections of electronic titles available. Originally the titles could be read through an online reader that would display one page of content at a time on the computer screen; searching and other features were available. Today, NetLibrary allows for downloading and reading content via Adobe Acrobat eBook Reader, one of the more popular reader applications. Adobe offers three reasons why a reader would want to read an e-book instead of a paper book:

> You can download eBooks to your laptop instead of lugging around heavy paper books. Plus the eBook's built-in dictionary is especially useful for reading technical and business materials. This is especially convenient for frequent travelers.
>
> If you are a student, you can download all your textbooks to your laptop so the laptop's all you need to bring to class. You can highlight passages, quickly search the text, make annotations, and create bookmarks just as you would with paper books.
>
> If you are anxious to read the latest bestseller, you can have the instant gratification of downloading and reading it immediately instead of waiting for it to be shipped.[8]

Many libraries provide access to e-books. Libraries have loaded MARC records from Project Gutenberg or NetLibrary into their catalogs with links to the full text.

Stand-alone e-book readers have been in development for some time. This dedicated hardware is designed to allow for easy carrying and better reading of text on a smaller, handheld screen. E-book reader models have come and gone with startling frequency. Patrons must make sure their system's software is compatible with what they wish to download, and this is no small task given the proliferation of formats. Names such as Rocket eBook, Everybook, e-bookman, and SoftBook have all been in the marketplace. Currently, Amazon's Kindle and Sony's Portable Reader are two of the most popular systems. Kindle has received a lot of publicity and has an impressive number of titles available, over 190,000—yet one year after its introduction, only 240,000 readers had been sold.[9]

E-book technology is changing rapidly. Many of the new cell phones can display e-books, and screen technology continues to improve. E-book technology has the potential to lessen the need for physical delivery, particularly in the areas of reference and best-seller titles. At this time, the number of titles available and patron interest in the technology are small; over time that will change, and as e-book use grows delivery should diminish.

Digitized Books

E-books were either created electronically at the point of publication or later transcribed to make online text available. Digitized books are basically photographs or picture captures of the contents of the pages of a printed book, map, photograph, or documents. These digital images are pulled together into digital libraries, which house and preserve the images and make the collections available for online access. Large numbers of libraries, museums, historical societies, newspaper publishers, and others are making copies of their collections available online—the Library of Congress Digital Library project, the New York Public Library NYPL Digital Gallery, and the British Library Digitization Project, to name a few.

Many of the items being digitized are not likely to be part of the typical shipment made by a library delivery system. Many of the digitized maps, older books, and photographs were rare or too fragile to start with and have never left their home archive or special collection. Other items such as historical photographs and local newspapers were not available prior to the cataloging and digitizing.

On the other hand, several new projects are digitizing entire university library collections that hold many items that are either checked out or loaned out and need delivery. The Open Knowledge commons has nineteen Massachusetts libraries signed up as well as MIT and the University of California system. Another nonprofit project is Europeana, which is providing access to Europe's digitized film material, photos, paintings, sounds, maps, manuscripts, books, newspapers, and archival papers. Entirely in the public domain, Europeana is funded by the European Commission, and it hopes to have ten million items online by 2010. Another American university project, HathiTrust (www.hathitrust.org), has 2.9 million digitized volumes as of this writing.

An example of a commercial digitization product is Google Book Search. Google is scanning one million items a year. According to Google, of the seven million books digitized, one million are "full preview" per agreements with publishers, one million are in the public domain, and the remaining five million are no longer in print or commercially available.[10] Copyright restrictions significantly limit the number of viewable pages. Public domain items can be downloaded, but Google claims that determining copyright ownership is difficult, so they tend to err toward keeping materials out of the public domain. For copyrighted materials, readers can sample various amounts of text, depending on the agreements Google has reached with publishers, and there are links in the record to where a patron can buy or borrow the item.

Depending on the type of material being converted, digitization has the potential to reduce the need for physical delivery significantly. Delivered items are likely to be mainly current and popular materials, but there is also a large amount of research material now moving physically between libraries. Research collections are being digitized and could be predicted to reduce physical delivery, particularly for academic-only delivery systems.

There could, however, be an opposite trend as well. These new search engines, such as Google Scholar or even Amazon.com, are making it easy to find exact content inside books for the first time ever. Google Book Search has a direct link to OCLC's WorldCat, allowing patrons to request a book from nearby libraries easily. It is possible that demand for delivery will increase as more of the contents of books become easier to find. Basically, there is no way of knowing the full impact of digitization at this time. This topic would make for a great research project in the near future.

Print-on-Demand

Print-on-demand (POD) is a technology that allows a copy of a new book or document to be printed on request. POD technology has revolutionized book publishing and printing. In the past, in order to be economically feasible a small book print run was a few thousand copies; now a single copy can be produced cheaply and with high-quality printing and binding. This still-evolving technology has revolutionized small and university presses, which are now printing and shipping some titles only when requested, rather than warehousing. Libraries are largely warehouse operations.

Products like Xerox's DocuShare are ending paper storage in offices all over the country. The Espresso Book Machine (EBM) is the size of a vending machine and can print books in a few minutes. Several universities' libraries (University of Michigan, Cornell University) are experimenting with the EBM to produce copies of their digitized works. An EBM project between the New York Public Library and New Orleans Public Library is allowing quick replacement of books lost via Hurricane Katrina.

It is interesting that increased digitization may be driving a demand for more printing. There is a long-running joke on the Internet, often attributed to a Xerox employee: "The paperless office will take over at about the same time as the paperless bathroom." Of all of the changes discussed in this section, POD is the hardest to gauge in terms of impact on library delivery. At this point in time, the impact is quite small, but we believe that as libraries figure out how best to integrate this technology into our practices it could have a huge impact as storage, retrieval, and shipping. Imagine a branch library the size of a vending machine–sized POD. The patron types in a book name, and a few minutes later a high-quality bound volume is available. If and when this vision is realized, it will not be only physical delivery but the concept of the library itself that has fundamentally changed.

Notes

1. Ann Cress, "The Latest Wave," *Library Journal* 129 (October 2004): 16.
2. "Reduced Transportation Holds at Its Best," *LINK Consortium News and Tips Newsletter,* July/August 2007.
3. Carol Pitts Diedrichs, "Designing and Implementing a Consortial Approval Plan: The OhioLINK Experience," *Collection Management* 24, no. 1 (2000): 15.
4. Kim Armstrong and Bob Nardini, "Making the Common Uncommon? Examining Consortial Approval Plan Cooperation," *Collection Management* 25, no. 3 (2001): 87.
5. James Burgett, Linda L. Phillips, and John M. Haar, *Collaborative Collection Development: A Practical Guide for Your Library* (Chicago: American Library Association, 2004).
6. Ann Beaubien, "ARL White Paper on Interlibrary Loan" (2007), www.arl.org/bm~doc/ARL_white_paper_ILL_june07.pdf.
7. Barbara Holton, Laura Hardesty, and Patricia O'Shea, *Academic Libraries: 2006 First Look,* NCES 2008-337 (U.S. Department of Education, National Center for Education Statistics, 2008).
8. "Why should I read eBooks instead of paper books?" (2008), www.adobe.com/support/ebookrdrfaq.html#whyread.
9. Erick Schonfeld, "We Know How Many Kindles Amazon Has Sold: 240,000," TechCrunch, August 1, 2008, www.techcrunch.com/2008/08/01/we-know-how-many-kindles-amazon-has-sold-240000/.
10. "Google Book Search," Wikipedia, http://en.wikipedia.org/wiki/Google_book_search#cite_note-pcworldscan-11 (retrieved December 2, 2008).

9
Managing Participating Libraries' Relationships

Valerie Horton

Managing participant relationships means handling both the efficient movement of library materials and the equally important interactions with staff from participating libraries. Communication, evaluation, policies, training, and statistical recordkeeping are all part of the manager's daily activities. Managing participant relationships is a complex task, and this section looks at several aspects of the process. The first is related to communication and connecting with participating libraries, and the second is related to providing a high-quality delivery service. Other elements a courier manager must deal with include user committees, training, marketing, and contractual agreements with participating libraries. At the core of all efforts in building and maintaining good relationships with participating libraries is a commitment to customer service.

COMMUNICATION

The participating library's staff member who deals directly and daily with the courier service is generally from the circulation, mailroom, or ILL department. Reaching these frontline staff directly through a complex library hierarchy can be difficult. It can also be difficult to communicate with the library workers in smaller libraries where a single staff member performs so many functions that he has little time to pay close attention to courier issues. Another area of communication difficulty arises when dealing with very large organizations, such as city governments or universities, where the library is only a small department. Hospitals, prisons, and federal buildings often have strong security measures that create both delivery and communication barriers.

There is a wide range of information that needs to be shared with frontline staff, including

- correcting labeling or packing errors
- changes in what can and cannot be delivered on a courier service
- unanticipated delays in services due to accidents or unexpected driver absence
- route changes
- weather delays or other road closures
- reports of lost or damaged materials
- driver misconduct

The list of communication needs is long; as a result, courier managers utilize many different methods to reach out to frontline staff in a timely fashion.

Manuals

Paper manuals are one of the most common communication tools used by courier managers. Manuals, some as long as thirty pages, are a mixture of standard operating procedures, instructional information, and reference sources. The manual often describes the mission and operations of the courier service and lists member libraries, fees, and courier personnel. Basically, a wide range of disparate information is jammed together in one paper resource.

A manual has two main advantages: all information about the service can be found in one place, and paper is easy to transport or download from a website. Conversely, there are several major drawbacks to paper manuals. They are difficult to update, paper is often misfiled or misplaced, and participating libraries may not regularly download the latest version. As a result, manuals are best used for information that rarely changes.

The following are topics found in the table of contents of a typical library courier manual:

- purpose or mission and governance of the courier system
- membership agreements and requirements to participate, including participant fees
- pickup and delivery schedules
- courier holidays or no-service days
- procedures for things such as packaging, labeling instructions, and handling lost or damaged items
- limits on financial compensation for lost or damaged items
- frequently asked questions
- how to order needed supplies

The manual does have the advantage of being the definitive source when disagreements occur over procedures. As long as the manual is widely distributed, there is at least the hope that the staff at the participating libraries will pay attention to the contents.

The paper manual, though common, is one of the least effective methods of distributing information to participating libraries. Library workers are too busy to use large, cumbersome print documents. A host of online tools are replacing reliance on paper manuals to communicate with participating libraries.

E-mail and Electronic Discussion Lists

Electronic mail allows information to be sent directly to a frontline staff member's computer account, which offers the courier manager several immediate advantages. First, it is a push technology that sends the information directly to the reader. Second, it is universally available in libraries. Finally, e-mail works especially well for short, to-the-point messages. For instance, a message that reads "Courier service in the southwest region will be delayed one hour due to a road closure on Highway 10" is easy to compose and gets right to the key point.

For small courier systems, it might be possible to maintain an e-mail address file with key contacts. For anyone who deals with more than a dozen contacts, e-mail address features are too cumbersome to manage. Most courier managers use electronic discussion lists to manage e-mail contacts. Once established, electronic discussion lists are often the fastest and most efficient source of communicating with critical frontline staff.

The problem with electronic discussion groups is that most library employees are already so inundated with e-mail information that they are reluctant to sign up for another list. In addition, getting word out about a new list, particularly in a larger consortium, can be difficult. One good method of gaining members on the courier's electronic discussion list is to require a first and second e-mail contact on the agreement used by a library to join or to continue to participate in a delivery service. One courier service solved a low-participation problem by leveraging a crisis into a communication success. The manager chose to use only the electronic discussion list to discuss a threat to the continued existence of the courier service. Within a short time, library staff demanded to be included in that electronic discussion list service.

Websites

Most library courier systems maintain a website with an array of useful information. Current sites span the spectrum from bare-bones, simple text information to information-rich, interactive tools. Standard sections found on most sites include mission and organizational descriptions, policies and procedures, contact information, list of participating libraries, pickup and delivery schedules, courier holidays, guides and training materials, FAQs and best-practices posters, forms and label printing, pricing and enrollment information, and electronic discussion group sign-up information. The more richly developed sites include promotional materials, maps, testimonials, start-up kits, statistics and reports, historical information, and a courier management system.

The advantages of a courier website are obvious. It provides a one-stop shop for delivery information. Websites are, however, pull-technology; they require the user to visit the site to retrieve the information. As a result, websites generally work poorly for emergency announcements. Further, maintaining current information online is generally not a top priority for busy courier managers.

An example of a full-featured website with strong use of graphics is SCLS's Delivery Service site (www.sclsdelivery.info). The site uses clear wording such as "Delivery Times," "Volume Statistics," and "Road and Weather" to aid retrieval of key information. The clean mix of graphics and text also helps readers navigate the site.

Many library courier delivery websites include human interest links, such as courier news, employment information, and courier history sections. It is easy to tell when the delivery service has paid attention to Internet communication. With the better-developed sites, the reader gets a feel that the courier service is substantial and cares about both professionalism and its image. We live in an era where library staff expect to find what they need fast and when they need it. A good, full-featured web page is a great way to get current information to most users in a manner that meets their expectations.

Newsletters

The day of the paper newsletter is passing, and this includes courier newsletters. As of this writing, a search of existing courier web pages found no courier-only newsletters. Some consortium-run courier systems do have newsletters, but information on the courier is a regular or occasional column among many other stories. Most courier systems use the Web as a de facto newsletter. Having a web section such as "What's New," "Courier News," "Courier Updates," or even just "Announcements" can serve the function once provided by newsletters.

Social Networking Tools

Blogs are websites that display messages added chronologically. Blogs are interactive, with most allowing the reader to respond to the writer's comments. Typically blogs are updated frequently and are intended for wide public readership. The problem with blogs is that there are so many available that it can be difficult to get key constituencies to read another one about the courier service. A blog can be either a pull or push medium. Readers can choose to treat a blog as a website and visit by entering an Internet address, or they may use a blog consolidator like Bloglines or My Yahoo, which pushes the information into a consolidated reader.

In general, blogs are not good for short-term emergency messages. They can, however, be a successful communication medium, particularly if the manager wishes to engage participating libraries in active dialogue. When significant changes are planned, such as introduction of a new code system, a blog allows two-way conversations. The courier manager can get a strong sense of the key issues affecting the delivery service by providing an interactive blog.

At this time, few courier managers are using blogs, and those who do use them more as a FAQ site than as an open communication medium. Other Web 2.0 tools that encourage social networking, like wikis and text messaging, are seldom if ever used by courier managers. To speculate about why courier managers have not moved more aggressively into social networking is guesswork. Fear of "unfettered negative" comments could play a role; lack of time is another likely reason. Two-way web communication tools are important. They make a statement about the open philosophy of the delivery service. Although courier managers have not fully grasped the need to incorporate these technologies, their integration is a matter of time.

In summary, courier managers should use a wide range of communication tools, choosing the most appropriate for each circumstance. The best courier systems use electronic discussion groups for emergency communication, websites for static information sharing, and social networking tools like blogs for two-way communication about issues.

USER COMMITTEES

A great way to develop two-way communication with library staff is to have a representational user committee. User committees appear to work best with six to ten members representing a diversity of libraries served. Committee members serve in an advisory capacity and can be instrumental in setting policies and developing procedures. The user committee can be an excellent informal communication tool that allows critical information exchange. The committee members are likely to share what they learn on the committee with others.

User committees have value beyond communication. They can keep mistakes from happening by catching design flaws in new projects and procedures before they are implemented. By serving as a conduit for problem resolution, these groups can help solve a problem before it gets too big to rectify easily. Having an active, engaged committee sends the signal to the wider library community that the courier service is open to participant input and responsive.

When developing a charge for the courier committee, the first question to ask is whether the committee is advisory or has direct responsibility for oversight of the daily activities of the courier service. This decision is usually based on the political situation. Whichever decision is made, this distinction needs to be indicated in the first sentence of the courier charge. An example of a charge that includes oversight could be "The Courier Committee is charged with the management of the courier system, including setting policy, oversight of the vendor contract, establishing type of stops, and pricing structure." Alternatively, the charge for an advisory committee could be "The Courier Committee serves as an advisory committee assisting the courier management team with setting policy and directions for the system." The first paragraph of the charge should include the larger context within which the committee operates and clearly indicate the committee's reporting hierarchy.

The charge should explain other duties as well. Does the committee set or recommend policies, prepare and release RFPs, negotiate contracts, establish billing structure, or evaluate the service? Whatever the duties, they should be listed so that committee members understand what is expected when they join. The committee's membership requirements should define representation of different constituencies. The terms of membership on the committee should also be spelled out and indicate whether additional terms can be granted.

Having a courier oversight committee is one of the smartest moves a courier manager can make. A well-run, active user committee is one of the keys to a successful courier service.

CONTRACTUAL RELATIONSHIP WITH PARTICIPATING LIBRARIES

A contract can be defined as an agreement between two or more parties whereby each party promises to do, or not to do, something; it is a transaction involving two or more individuals whereby each has reciprocal rights to demand performance of what is promised. The courier service agrees to deliver and pick up materials for a specified number of days per week to a library that has agreed to participate. This relationship is often clarified in a legal contract between the two parties. The main reason to have a contract is that it provides a place where the agreement between the two parities is clearly stated, which helps reduce the chance of conflict or legal action.

It is also possible, and likely preferable, to use a service agreement between the library and courier service instead of a contract. A contract deals with terms, penalties, indemnification, and finances that bind the parties and is often written in formal legal language. A service agreement tends to have less-binding legal status. Agreements are often good faith documents committing two parties to an ongoing relationship to provide services or to follow accepted procedures and make prompt payments. On one extreme, there are courier services in this country for which the invoice serves as the entire agreement between the two parties. Each library courier service must decide what level of legal protection suits its operating philosophy.

For some libraries, the courier service is one of several consortium-purchased services, such as online catalog access or database purchases. In these situations, the courier contract is typically part of a larger contractual relationship. For a few libraries the governing body, such as a multicampus university system, runs a service and the courier is simply part of the overall campus infrastructure. In such cases no separate contractual relationships are required.

Whatever the contractual situation, the courier service needs to know the following from participant libraries: name, address, membership category (if part of a larger consortium), pickup location within the building, and hours/days when delivery is possible. Other items to consider include special instructions that are important when dealing with state or federal buildings, prisons, or hospitals, such as instructions that give the information necessary to deal with guard posts and other security measures. Contact information should include a primary and secondary contact name, phone, and e-mail. The schedule of delivery is important for small public libraries, which may not be open five days a week. If schools are involved, the information should include whether the school is open on a nine- or twelve-month basis.

From a courier manager's perspective, the fewer invoicing options the better. The service agreement holds the library to paying at set times only. Although it is always preferable to having a single invoicing schedule, it is not always possible. Some systems allow monthly, annual, semiannual, or quarterly billing, which can be expensive and time consuming to maintain. Given the different fiscal years used by libraries (e.g., academic, July–June; public, January–December), offering alternate invoicing is often frequently necessary, but holding the variation to a minimum is desirable.

Figure 9.1 is an example of the type of language found in a courier agreement. The language is designed to protect the courier service by specifying that participants follow the posted policies and procedures and ship only acceptable items. This courier service takes limited responsibility for lost or damaged materials and does not reimburse for missed stops. Each service agreement is different, but all, whether a contract or an agreement, should be legally reviewed to make sure the manager is protecting assets of the organization.

TRAINING

Several issues covered earlier in this book mention the importance of training, such as how to follow packaging procedures, request lost book refunds, and the like. As with communications with participating libraries, the courier website is an excellent vehicle for providing just-in-time, 24/7 training. Courier training falls into two main categories: the big-picture issues, such as statewide or consortium-wide resource sharing; and the details of how to use the courier service, such as labeling and packing.

_____ Library Courier

Request for Service Form

The _____ (participant library)
requests courier service for the period January 1, 20__, through December
31, 20__. By initiating this request, the participant understands that the
courier service will make every reasonable effort to ensure that materials are
delivered reliably by its courier contractor. **However, this service assumes
no responsibility whatsoever for lost, missing, or damaged materials
transported by the courier.**

The undersigned, on behalf of the participant library, has read the
guidelines and procedures for courier service. The participant will make every
reasonable effort to comply with these guidelines and procedures, which may
be updated from time to time. Participant acknowledges that its sole remedy
for lost, damaged, or missing items is to seek recovery from the courier
service as provided in the guidelines and procedures. An occasional missed
stop, whether the reason is weather, traffic, vehicle, or some other problem,
is not reimbursed.

The undersigned warrants that he/she has full authority to execute this
request on behalf of the participant library.

_____   _____

Signature of Authorized Agent for Participant Library   Date

_____

Typed or printed name of Authorized Agent

Figure 9.1   Example courier service agreement

Because physical delivery is perceived as somewhat separate from typical
library duties, explanations of how delivery fits into the wider world of patron services are often necessary, particularly for new or lower-level library staff. Courier
managers have found it necessary to explain exactly what resource sharing is, how
it works, and how the library courier contributes to the enterprise.

Some courier systems have developed multimedia explanations of resource
sharing and physical delivery. On the Web, these systems are available 24/7 and
usually take ten to fifteen minutes to read. MINITEX from Minnesota uses a light-

hearted slideshow narrated by "Del the Book" (www.minitex.umn.edu/delivery/). The Colorado Library Consortium has developed a "Resource Sharing 101" tutorial (www.clicweb.org/continuing_education/tutorials/resourcesharingmain.php) that uses Captivate software to provide a host of graphics, voiceover narrative, and videos clips to explain how all of Colorado's various resource-sharing and ILL systems interact with the statewide courier.

The courier manager must first establish *why* you need resource sharing. After that, the second type of training explains the nitty-gritty of how to interact with the specific courier service. This hands-on how-to-use-the-courier training is the more common type and tends to come in more formats. The point of this type of training is to explain how library staff should interact with the courier service's established policies and procedures. Most of these training materials are simple written procedures that outline specific tasks step by step. Written instructions of this type tend to focus on the concrete, such as "Use only sticky labels Avery 6164 or size 64."

Some library courier systems do incorporate graphic or full video productions to demonstrate actions required by participant libraries. The Colorado Library Consortium's online tutorial "Courier 101" uses the same Captivate software as "Resource Sharing 101" mentioned above. This tutorial gets specific in how to find courier codes, create labels, and package materials for shipping and uses voiceover explanations and step-by-step visuals to demonstrate how procedures should be followed (www.clicweb.org/continuing_education/tutorials/courier101main.php).

Another tried-and-true technique is the in-person workshop. Many courier services send a courier staff person to a new participating library during start-up to train library staff on correct procedures. For long-standing members, phone calls and e-mails are more common for refresher training. Many courier managers take advantage of consortium or state conferences to hold short information sessions. These face-to-face sessions have the added advantage of allowing participant feedback.

Special mention should be made of customer service training for frontline courier staff. The customer service employee who interacts with the staff from participating libraries is often in a stressful situation. When problems occur, and problems always occur, the person who answers the phone at the courier office must be professional and calm in the face of whatever problem or disaster has occurred in the field. The frontline staff person should be enthusiastic about excellent customer service and should be offered training or encouragement to maintain high-quality service over time.

PUBLIC RELATIONS AND MARKETING

Some courier managers have a locked-in set of participating libraries and have no need to add new libraries. Other managers are looking to expand their delivery service. In both cases, public relations and marketing are required. If the courier manager does not tell the story of the courier service, the story will be told by others, and perhaps that story may not be as positive as would be desired. Public relations and marketing shape participants' attitudes about the courier, and they are important tools in the manager's kit.

Most courier managers are not marketing experts; they either rely on the organization's marketing staff or hire outside experts. It is beyond the scope of this book to elaborate the elements of a good marketing campaign, but a few key points can be made. Too many library courier services do not brand their product. Without graphics, a logo, or some form of character association, the courier service can seem bland and uninspiring. The best courier marketing tools make full use of color, texture, product selection, and branding techniques.

The aforementioned Del the Book from MINITEX is a good example of visual marketing. The Illinois Delivery System uses a strong black "ILDS" intersected by a bold purple arrow, creating a logo that gives the sense of movement or delivery. Wisconsin's SCLS uses a standard picture of a truck as its logo with the name of the delivery service printed on the side of the truck. The Michigan Library Consortium has a delightful graphic of a moose. New York's NYLINK LAND delivery service also uses a truck, but in a more stylized fashion the word "LAND" is incorporated as part of the actual image of the truck, again suggesting movement.

Finding a logo, image, or picture that captures the value of the courier service helps create a positive attitude toward the service with patrons and government funding sources. Alert managers look for opportunities to tell the best possible delivery story.

The best-run courier services make heavy use of electronic communication, well-developed websites, customer training, and marketing. The importance of tasks like these is often undervalued by consortium or system directors; yet another burden on the courier manager is to educate her superiors about the importance of these bottom-line tasks.

10

Managing the Delivery Service

Valerie Horton, Lisa Priebe, and Melissa Stockton

In many ways, managing a courier service is similar to any duty a typical library manager performs. There are budgets to be created, staff to be hired, and supplies to be purchased. A courier service needs to conform to standard business practices such as having a mission and goals, management systems, recordkeeping, evaluations, and planning. In the next few sections we look at standard practices related to managing a courier service, then the final section covers services to special populations and potential growth paths into new activities using a courier service.

MISSIONS, GOALS, AND PLANNING

Mission and goal statements provide both participating and potential member libraries with a clear concept of what the courier service is and what it hopes to become in the future. A mission statement tells what the organization is, why it exists, and why it should continue to exist. The best mission statements are short, clear, and memorable. Here are a few examples:

The Interlibrary Delivery Service (IDS) of Pennsylvania's purpose is to provide a cost-effective efficient delivery service linking all types of libraries to support timely resource sharing throughout the Commonwealth of Pennsylvania.

Trans-Amigos Express (TAE) is the Amigos-wide courier service offering low-cost, rapid pickup and delivery of ILL items among participating libraries.

The Colorado Library Courier provides delivery service to participating libraries of all types across the State. We are committed to providing reliable and efficient courier service to participating libraries.

These mission statements are to the point and tell the reader why the courier service exists.

Goal statements are targets to be achieved within a certain time frame. They are future oriented, setting the direction for the organization to go. Library delivery services typically have three goals: low-cost delivery, rapid delivery, and widespread library participation. In practice, these three goals are often part of the mission statement. An example of this type of mission statement: "The courier provides low-cost, one- to two-day delivery of all types of library materials to the ACME Consortium."

Goal statements should stand alone, separate from the mission statement. Library courier service managers want their service to be reliable, to have polite and professional drivers, and to be accurate in meeting established pickup times. An example of such a goal statement: "Our goal is to reach by 2010 an on-time delivery rate of 99 percent, weather and road conditions permitting; our school library participation in the courier service will increase 10 percent in the next fiscal year." Most organizations have three to five goals. These goals are often broken into achievable tasks. An example of a task for increasing the goal of school participations: "By October 30, all nonparticipating schools will receive a new member brochure and a follow-up phone call."

Mission and goal statements are usually created as part of a planning process. Delivery services need concrete plans to deal with the purchase of large-ticket items like a new vehicle or automated material handling/sorting system. Plans can be long or short term, but the most important part of the plan is the process of thinking through future directions. Involving user committees and other library staff is critical to an open process that explores a wide range of options.

Once the plan is complete, the manager should put it on the website, incorporate the tasks into individual work plans, and routinely check progress. Updates can be made on anniversary dates or as circumstances change. The most important goals for all library delivery systems remain providing fast, accurate, professional, and timely delivery service to participating libraries.

POLICIES AND PROCEDURES

Courier managers, like other library managers, use policies and procedures to instruct and guide use of the delivery service. Courier policies should emphasize the importance of rules, be long term in scope, and be consulted when decisions are made. Courier policies often are approved by a governing body or board and tend not to be subject to frequent revisions. In comparison, courier procedures are the tools used to carry out the policies. Procedures are step-by-step directions guiding recurring action. Procedures are helpful to employees and participants because they often break down complex activities into easy-to-follow steps. Procedures are subject to frequent change as managers attempt to improve efficiency.

Policies

Courier policies are usually the rules that dictate who is allowed into the service, how much it costs, and what may be shipped. In a consortium, the bylaws typically give the consortium's governing board final policymaking authority. In academic library systems, there is usually a hierarchical structure, with approval coming from a director's or dean's council. In either case, the process typically has the courier managers writing early drafts of the policies, and then the governing entity reviews, edits, and approves the policies.

For services that charge for delivery, one of the most important policies is price setting. Pricing policies often involve extensive negotiation among participating members, state governing funders, or other involved parties. Setting pricing for the upcoming year is often one of the manager's main concerns, particularly in a time of rapidly fluctuating fuel prices, as has happened since 2000.

A typical pricing policy might include membership fee information. For example: "Participant courier dues are determined annually by the Board. The level of use in the previous year by the members will be the basis for setting pricing." Examples of other policy statements: "If a member library also subscribes to the basic database package and uses the interlibrary loan subsystem, a 5 percent discount on membership fees will be included for courier participation"; or "For all new members after membership approval is gained, an estimated delivery charge will be created by the Board."

Policies commonly found in library delivery services cover eligibility, service area, types of libraries that can join, types of materials that can be shipped; and insurance and liability requirements. It is not uncommon to find combined policies on lost and damaged materials, even though the two events are likely from different causes and typically have different resolutions. The set of policies reflects the unique political situation of each courier operation.

Many policies contain clear statements about the responsibilities of the participating libraries. For instance, a policy could include one of the following sentences: "Participating libraries are required to abide by all service policies and procedures"; or "The local library is responsible for acquiring appropriate shipping supplies, excluding containers." It is important that the policies clearly state what is required of everyone involved.

Policies establish how problems are going to be handled before they happen. Enforcing the policies equitably and in good faith is part of the courier manager's job. Making sure the participating libraries know about policies is the hardest part of the process. The courier manager must make sure that policies are explained to new members and that established members are routinely reminded. Policies, though not given to frequent change, should be reviewed and updated on a regular basis at least every year or two.

Lost Materials Policies

Every courier loses materials on rare occasions, and policies are needed to clarify responsibilities in those circumstances. These policies protect both the courier and the member libraries. In multitype consortia, lost materials in particular can become a source of misunderstanding and conflict. A common perception among library staff is that the "other type" of library always loses my library's books. This division tends to play out along the standard public versus academic library lines. Though loss rates may vary by type of library, they are typically quite low.

The main problem with lost material is identifying where exactly the item got lost. Did it disappear before it left the lending library? Did it get lost en route, in the sorting process, or at the borrowing library? There is almost no way to know, and experienced courier managers have learned that most lost materials are eventually found at the borrowing or lending library. MINITEX solved this problem by moving to a "secure the tub" system in which all totes are closed by zip-ties (plastic locking strips) before they leave the library. Confidence in the system increased once this practice was put in place.

Some systems have chosen to deal with the issue by having no financial remuneration for lost books. These systems have replaced time-consuming and complex reimbursement systems with yearly book searches. A printout of all books lost in the system is sent out once a year or so. These lists are searched and, not surprisingly, most materials are found to be misshelved at either the lending or borrowing library.

Alternatively, some pay for all lost books with no questions asked. This pay-without-question system has advantages in the area of public relationships, but it requires that more fees be collected from member libraries to cover the lost funds. Some luckier systems have managed to get a clause written into the vendor contract according to which the vendor pays for all lost books whether they were the cause or not. For courier services that use commercial services such as UPS or FedEx, their individual package tracking means the vendor pays if an item is lost.

Without piece tracking, a courier manager cannot determine whether an item was lost at the sending or receiving library or during transit on the courier. No matter how the courier service chooses to handle lost books, the process is time consuming and often politically complex.

Damaged Materials Policies

There is an unwritten law of delivery, namely, that library materials will get damaged. As a rule, libraries do not allow severely damaged materials to circulate to patrons, let alone be lent to another library. In most cases, damage occurs either in transit or at the sorting facility. The reality is that drivers do not always properly seal bins or close bags in bad weather. Drivers spill coffee or drop packages onto the muddy ground. Libraries increase the likelihood of damage when they do not pack materials correctly in containers or bags. Damage policies typically determine when and how the courier service takes responsibility for a mishap. Most policies spell out what is reimbursed (books, CDs, DVDs, VHSs) and what is not (equipment, rare, valuable, or personal items).

Most courier services request that damage be reported immediately on discovery. Typically the courier service asks the library if the materials can be repaired. If the item cannot be repaired, it is usually sent to the courier for inspection and reimbursement based on contractual schedules.

Procedures

Procedures are essential to the courier manager; they provide the critical how-to necessary for running an efficient organization. Many procedures are connected to labeling and packing material for delivery. Even the smallest, most informal courier operations have some form of packaging procedures. Most packaging procedures are step-by-step instructions, as the example in figure 10.1 illustrates.

Courier managers specify to the smallest detail which packaging, labels, and materials groupings are allowed; for instance, one courier system specifies that only rubber band size 64 or 117B may be used. Courier drivers are often instructed not to pick up materials that do not meet requirements. Although this meticulous attention to detail can seem nitpicky, given the volume of materials most couriers move, procedures are needed for efficient function.

For the most part, each courier system has developed its own policies, procedures, guidelines, and best practices. This lack of uniformity stands in sharp contrast to ILL, which has the Interlibrary Loan Code for the United States, approved through ALA's RUSA in January 2001. Several groups are looking at sharing information between courier providers, but we are a long way from developing uniform standards for delivery.

GUIDELINES FOR USING PINK INTERSYSTEM ROUTING LABELS

Step 1

Check the Wisconsin Libraries' Delivery Service Network List* to see if the receiving library is a member of the Network. If not, then you find another means of shipment, e.g., US Postal Service or commercial parcel/courier services.

*The list can be located by clicking on the "Delivery Network" icon. The list of the libraries participating in the Wisconsin Libraries' Delivery Service Network has two columns.

Step 2

Fill in the **For:** on the pink intersystem routing label.
Use the left-hand column, Delivery Network Member of the Wisconsin Libraries' Delivery Service Network list.

Step 3

Fill in the **To:** on the pink intersystem routing label.
Use the right-hand column, System Delivery Hub of the Wisconsin Libraries' Delivery Service Network list.

Figure 10.1   South Central Library System shipping guidelines

COURIER MANAGEMENT SYSTEMS

A courier management system is a digital tool to help administer a library courier service. It can make delivery operations simpler and quicker while making the process more transparent and easier for member libraries and management staff. Some common functions for library staff include looking up codes for other libraries and printing routing slips. Information stored in the system can transform the job of the courier manager from one that involves multiple spreadsheets, files, and sticky notes to a job where contact information and statistical reports are kept in a centralized database accessed through a single interface. Although moving to a courier management system may involve a large amount of staff time, once in place it makes the work of running a courier service easier and more efficient.

Libraries using a courier service have a variety of needs that all center on moving material between libraries and communication with participants. The features in the courier management system need to be intuitive and help library staff navigate the required courier policies. It is imperative the system be flexible enough to allow libraries to utilize their own method for processing materials while maintaining systemwide policies and procedures.

A fully functional system would include the following features for the member libraries:

- create routing slips and labels and easily print them out singly or in batches
- find courier code or address information
- find contact information at other libraries
- access instructions for preparing items for shipment or tutorials
- update contact information

The courier manager needs not just access to library contact information but the ability to modify that information on a regular basis. Managers must determine the information needed to describe the members of the group. This may include organization names, addresses, and contacts as well as any specialized information such as interorganizational relationships or affiliate groups. When moving to an automated system, it is important to preserve as much of the information from data files as possible. The information in current management files must be reviewed, updated, and made as consistent as possible. Inconsistencies can mean that data cannot be loaded, are loaded incorrectly, or affect the accuracy of statistical reports.

In addition to member library contacts, information specific to delivery schedules is also required. Information ensuring delivery, such as courier code, route name/number, service start/end dates, closed dates, and delivery days should all be available in the system. If you are implementing an integrated courier management system, it is a good time to review and revamp all the different reports and statistics currently in use. A new system should give the manager options regarding formats, timing, and availability. With an online system, some reports may no longer be required, since libraries can access the information at any time.

The courier management system should provide the manager with all the reports needed for member libraries, governing bodies, and courier service partners. Any report package should be flexible and allow the managing organization to select the criteria for the report as well as the fields for output. The reports should be viewable online, at the least. Downloading to Excel and other output capabilities that would allow manipulation of the report data are highly desirable.

Most courier managers invoice member libraries directly, though in some consortia the courier is one service among many and may be included as part of a larger bill for services. For those who do invoice directly, the billing module of any courier management system should be customizable and flexible. Using the system, the manager should be able to determine the costs for each library, payment status, and any identifying information required for the billing process. The system should allow either the ability to create and send invoices or to output the information for use in other billing systems. Historical information should be maintained and made available.

Another important tool is a module to track lost and damaged items. As with other features, allowing flexibility in implementing options is important. The ability to enter lost or damaged items into the system should be controlled so that only authorized personnel can report an issue. Member libraries should be able to pull up a list of their own lost and damaged items. Automatic communication tools reduce the level of manual tasks required to move items through the lost and damaged processes.

Finally, one of the most valuable features of a courier management system is the ability to target communications to specific individuals, routes, or groups of participating libraries. The manager should be able to quickly select an individual or a group listed in the courier management system for an e-mail distribution. The system may offer automatic e-mail that informs people when specific changes are made in the delivery system, such as a change in route times or courier delivery days.

Developing a Courier Management System

Each organization has different reasons for considering a courier management system solution. Think about the following questions to guide your decision:

- Does the courier manager struggle to provide timely and accurate reports to management concerning usage, problem tracking, and membership?
- Does the courier manager rely on multiple spreadsheets, paper files, and databases to manage the current courier process?
- Is the number of addressing errors on sorting and routing slips causing an undue burden on the courier manager and affecting delivery time of material?
- Does the courier manager struggle to find a way to communicate with member libraries individually, with a subset of libraries, or with the group as a whole?
- Is it difficult for libraries and the courier manager to report and track lost and damaged materials or problems with delivery?
- Is library contact information out of date, incomplete, or difficult to keep current?
- Will the savings gained in higher productivity and fewer errors offset the cost of development and implementation of a new system?

Answering yes to three or more of these questions may be enough to convince an organization that a courier management system should be investigated.

Courier management staff are responsible for overseeing the development process of a courier management system. The steps involved are the same whether the system is developed in-house or by a third party.

The organization begins the process by establishing system requirements for the new software. System requirements are identified by evaluating current processes and procedures and identifying priorities. The following questions help identify the areas that benefit most from automation:

- Which pieces of the process are the most important to the management staff and which are most important to the member libraries?
- Are there unfilled needs a new system could fill?
- Which areas of your current practices take the most time to explain to members?
- Which area gets the most complaints from users?
- What information is unnecessarily "hidden" in your current procedures?

- Which parts and how much of your management activities do you want to automate? A list of libraries and courier codes on a static web page may work for some, but the more libraries involved, the less helpful a web page may be for users.
- Should libraries be allowed to update their own contact information? How is your contact information stored?
- Is it easy to communicate with a single person or everyone on a route?
- How do you keep track of library closed dates?
- How do you make library-specific information available to other libraries and to your courier service provider?
- How do you handle trouble tickets?
- What kind of follow-up system do you utilize to make sure the problems have been resolved?
- What kind of billing mechanism do you have?

The basic information the manager is attempting to understand is which questions the staff must answer about the service on a daily basis, and what information they want to track and have available for reporting.

Once the system requirements have been detailed, the organization must decide to build or buy a system. The following questions serve as a decision-making guide:

- Do systems exist that could be modified for organizational needs?
- Do staff have the necessary skills to build or maintain a system?
- What is the budget for developing and implementing a solution?
- What maintenance costs need to be considered?
- Would the system be implemented in phases to spread out the cost?
- Are there other systems the courier management system must interface with?

Regardless of the decision to build or buy, before proceeding the manager needs a thorough understanding of current data and work processes. A process and workflow review brings together several people with different skills and knowledge, including a systems analyst, the courier manager, and key internal staff and end users. Data conversion must also be planned to avoid extensive manual data entry. Be aware that converted data may require a thorough cleanup. Data cleanup and testing are both time consuming and essential to developing a workable system.

A process for communicating problems to the developers should be established before testing begins. A copy of the original converted data should be kept

COURIER MANAGEMENT SYSTEM: A CASE STUDY

The Colorado Library Consortium (CLiC) is a nonprofit organization that connects libraries across Colorado regardless of library type or size. The organization is best known for the management of a statewide courier that moves more than five million items between 390 libraries each year.

Until mid-2007, the day-to-day management of the courier was handled with a seven-year-old Microsoft Access database, plus four spreadsheets and an assortment of paper files, sticky notes, and e-mails. Participating libraries found courier code lists and lost item reports on the website. An online form was used to notify the courier manager of a lost or damaged item.

Several issues plagued the system: communication difficulties between libraries and the courier manager; tracking courier problems; inability to provide accurate statistical reports to management; a database that contained inaccurate data; a cumbersome, labor-intensive process; and library finding aids that were difficult to develop and time consuming to maintain.

Our goal was to cut staff time required to manage the courier while enhancing the level of service to libraries. CLiC's staff could not undertake the development of a web-based software project of this magnitude. The solution was to work with a development partner, Quipu Group. Three levels of system features, based on the level of security, were developed. The functions available to all library staff without a login included the ability to search for a courier code, produce a printable courier code report and routing slips, and link to information about the courier. The second level of security requires a login and password and is available to selected library staff. Users may change library contact information, notify the courier manager of lost or damaged items, and look up contact information for other participating libraries. The highest level of security is for the courier manager, who can update any library's information, create ad hoc reports and send group e-mail, track billing, and maintain system settings.

Communication concerning the availability of a new system began five months before system release. It cannot be overstressed how important this communication was to the success of the project. It gave the library community ample time to hear why the changes were being made and the ability to ask questions and suggest changes. Libraries received information via user meetings, individual library visits, electronic discussion groups, and direct mailing.

Library staff from member institutions participated in the system testing. Testers were given little training and asked to evaluate the ease of use in addition to the functionality of the system. Based on their comments, the following training tools were created: a fact sheet describing key system functions, an FAQ, and an online help system. Most implementation issues and questions were addressed individually, and when warranted library site visits were conducted by CLiC staff.

In a recent organizational survey, the courier was ranked high by the library community. The courier management system is a part of that success. Key elements to success include keeping the library community informed from start to finish, involving key library community members during development, a thorough data cleanup, and an educated and knowledgeable courier staff.

separate from the data that are being used to test. Problems found in the system need to be communicated in a detailed manner and a tracking mechanism created to monitor when issues are fixed or identified as enhancements to be added later.

Consider user training needs well in advance of the system implementation. Training can occur in many forms, from Help files that are part of the finished product to in-person, hands-on training classes offered in locations across the service area or as an online tutorial that can be viewed at the user's convenience.

The key to a smooth implementation is communication. An organization should begin discussing changes that affect libraries as early in the process as possible. If a completely new system is being developed, library staff must be given an opportunity to understand the benefits of undertaking a development project, be able to voice concerns, and understand how it will improve the service they and their patrons receive. Remember that communication continues after implementation. Look for libraries that need additional help in learning the system or understanding why the changes were implemented in the first place. Some hands-on training and face-to-face communication may be necessary and should be planned for before it is needed.

Enhancements to the base system can be identified at every phase of the development cycle. The key is to capture these ideas and after implementation have staff prioritize them. It is suggested that up to 10 percent of the initial system development budget be set aside for enhancements. No matter how thorough the gathering of requirements, enhancements are always found later in the development life cycle.

Do not underestimate the time and effort it takes to move to a courier management system from a system of sticky notes, spreadsheets, and folders of paper. Once in place, however, it will make the work of running a courier service simpler and more cost efficient and will improve service to libraries.

MANAGEMENT OF STATISTICS

One of the primary reasons to keep statistics is to prove that use of the delivery system justifies the expense. Inexpensive delivery is a winning argument with the government officials, college officers, and taxpayers. Statistics are also used to get accurate pricing for participating libraries, for contract negotiations with potential vendors, to help determine need or demand for service, to understand demographics, for inventory purposes, and to inform decision making for routes, size of trucks, and number of bins.

The ideal statistical management system would count every item shipped, keep track of how long it took to reach its destination, and calculate exact costs of each transaction. For those who are handling millions of items on tight budgets, such elaborate statistics are infeasible from the perspective of both time and finances. As a result, several different ways of keeping snapshots of statistics have been developed.

Software Counts

One of the most significant counts is the number of items shipped by the courier service, and there are several different methods for estimating this number. One of the easiest is to get an exact count from the online ILL software used by participating libraries, but such easy answers are available only when a courier service is tied to a single online catalog and a single ILL system. Most libraries use multiple ILL systems and are involved in numerous resource-sharing and delivery systems. When different ILL systems, online catalog interfaces, and delivery methods interact, exact counts are rarely possible to tabulate.

Tote, Bin, or Package Counts

One of the more commonly gathered statistic is a simple tote, bin, or package count. This is a count of the number of totes, bins, or packages picked up and delivered each day at every location along a route. The information is recorded on simple logs sheets, as shown in figure 10.2. The obvious disadvantage of this system is that the manager does not know how many items are in each bin, package,

LIBRARY DELIVERY SERVICE: ROUTE 7					
DATE	TIME	DRIVER'S INITIALS	# OF TOTES DELIVERED	# OF TOTES PICKED UP	LIBRARY STAFF SIGNATURE

Figure 10.2   Example stop log

or tote. Estimates can be used, but if one tote can have thirty books and another two, determining accurate numbers is impossible.

Items Counts

For courier services that use national carriers such as FedEx, it is easy to get an exact item shipment count. Some smaller systems also count every package delivered, and this number is used to determine the library's fee. With these systems, participating libraries are usually required to log onto a website and report the number of packages sent and received on a daily, weekly, or monthly basis. The honor system works in almost all cases, with managers trusting that libraries are reporting accurate usage numbers. It is impossible to count each package if the service is delivering more than a million items a year. As a result, exact item count systems are almost always the smaller library delivery systems.

A variation on exact item counts makes use of average item counts per tote, bin, or package to come up with a standard number. This can be done by a manual item count of a sample number of totes, bins, or packages. A table can be created on which a library staff person or driver can enter the number of totes, bins, or packages sent. From that data an estimated number of items are automatically calculated. The actual number of items may vary based on the size and type of material shipped, but the standard numbers allow for a working estimate. Another variation is to determine an average weight of each tote, tub, or bin. Like the method of average items per container, the number of containers can be entered into a table to calculate automatically the estimated weight of shipments. This method can be used when pricing is based on weight.

Although these methods may or may not get accurate delivery counts, they all allow for reasonably accurate comparisons between different participating libraries. It is unlikely that one library would be over- or undercharged, since all libraries are reporting based on the same tables. In addition, the courier manager also has a defensible number to report for overall system deliveries.

Sampling

Another method is a sample count of totes or bins for a limited period. This count can take place once or twice a year, quarterly, or at random intervals. In these cases, forms are available online that libraries use for one week or so to count the number of items placed in bins and received from bins. It is not uncommon with this type of sampling to count other things as well, including types of materials being sent or how long it takes for individual items to arrive. This kind of sampling gives the courier manager trend data that can be critical for extrapolating about overall system usage.

Whichever statistical counts are taken, it is most important to use roughly the same counts year after year. Trend data that look at usage over time can be crucial indicators for planning and budget negotiations.

EVALUATING THE DELIVERY SERVICE

Evaluation is an ongoing activity, and numerous aspects of the delivery service require assessment. Evaluation allows the manager to determine how well the service is doing and provides the information needed to make improvements. The task is to ask what has worked and why, and what has not worked and why. A well-established culture of assessment demonstrates accountability and shows that the manager is committed to both gaining input from participants and improving the efficiency and effectiveness of the delivery service.

Most evaluation measures are either measures of quantity or measures of quality. Quantitative measures attempt to gain accurate counts of activities: the what, where, and when questions. Quantitative analyses include how many items move, how many are damaged or lost, and how long delivery takes. Qualitative measures are based more on human behavior or perception. Qualitative measures are looking at the why and how of decision making and judgment. For a delivery service, that means determining what is an acceptable level of customer service and asking whether participating libraries' needs and expectations are being met.

Quantitative Measures

There are times when a delivery manager feels that all she does is gather numbers, but what the numbers show is critical in providing information about the delivery service. The following are examples of quantitative measures:

Lost or damaged books counts. The logistics industry considers it a major problem if more than 0.025 percent of materials are lost or damaged during transition. Any number higher than that is a red flag requiring immediate reexamination of procedures and processes.

Delivery speed. There are many different methods to determine how long an item takes to get from one site to another. Most courier services define an acceptable time range, usually 24–48 hours, after pickup by the driver. For the most part, checking every delivery is unrealistic, so many library delivery services do either regularly scheduled or randomly assigned spot checks of how long a package takes to be delivered.

Route speed. Do trained drivers on the same route take the same time? This measure creates a personal accountability metric.

Missorts and miscoding. Though somewhat hard to measure, tracking the number of complaints regarding missorts (items sent to the wrong library) and miscoding (incorrectly filled-out shipping labels) over time can give valuable information on the problems participants face.

Qualitative Measures

Qualitative measures are often harder to gather than quantitative measures, for the manager must try to assess what people think. The following are examples:

Customer service. A way to find out if there are problems with drivers that are going unnoticed is to survey participants and ask about their experiences. Questions can also be asked about how the office staff deals with problem reports, billing issues, and other day-to-day service issues.

Needs met. Participants have attitudes about the level of service they expect from the delivery service. Surveying to find out if the courier service is meeting those needs can help measure the strength of the organization. A service quality system can help the manager determine the gap between the service provided and the expectation of their participating libraries.[1]

Problem handling. How well are problems being resolved? Simple techniques, like requiring courier personnel to ask at the end of each customer encounter whether the customer felt their service needs were meet and then recording the answer, can be a powerful way to maintain customer service excellence.

One of the most effective evaluation tools is the short and simple survey. There are three questions that can be asked in many different formats and venues: What are we doing well? What can we do better? What aren't we doing that we should be doing? These questions can be asked with a simple online survey, a postcard survey, at meetings or conferences, or with a phone call. The three questions cover a huge range of information, and a courier manager would do well to pay close attention to the responses.

The courier manager should strive to create a culture of assessment. Whenever the manager meets with a group of participating libraries, ask how the service is going. Add a permanent website problem report and courier evaluation section. Pay special attention to comments written by participants. Bring small groups together to brainstorm what is working well, what could be improved, and what new services should be provided. There are limitless ways of evaluating the courier service; the best managers are always looking for new ways to incorporate assessment into every aspect of the service.

EXPANDING COURIER SERVICES

The "Grow or Die" motto is the inspiration behind many successful businesses and an appropriate one for the library courier manager as well. Once library courier services are running smoothly, policies are in place, training is ongoing, and the website is up and complete, it is time to look for growth opportunities. Libraries grow by offering more and better services to their patrons, and the courier manager has a part to play in the process.

Institutional Libraries

Service to some institutional libraries brings several unique challenges for the courier manager. Most institutional libraries have limited materials budgets, and resource sharing is a good way to provide materials to an underserved population. However, institutional libraries tend to be net borrowers because of their limited collection, and this can cause problems for systems that attempt to even out or load-level between borrowing and lending. That said, most larger libraries prefer unbalanced lending to having to ship anything via the USPS.

Although all libraries are becoming more security conscious, nothing compares to the security requirement necessary for delivery to prisons. Special badges are universally required by drivers delivering to prisons, and substantial paperwork usually must be filed with the department of corrections before those badges are issued. Even to interact at the guard station outside the fenced parameter, extra security checks have to be made on delivery drivers. Drivers end up having extra security checks beyond the typical motor vehicle checks, and drivers must be on the "approved list" before they can deliver materials. Gaining access for backup drivers when the main driver is unavailable can be a real headache for courier managers. For security, speed, and driver safety reasons, it is best to request that totes be delivered to the guard station or another area where prisoners are not allowed access.

Archives and Special Collections

Several states including California and Wisconsin have developed systems to ship rare and special collection materials between libraries. This on-campus delivery allows scholars to study rare primary source materials without substantial travel. The materials are shipped to another archive or special collection, where meticulous standards are maintained to handle often fragile and usually unique items. Special arrangements have been worked out by all participating entities well in advance of any materials shipment.

Special boxes or other delivery containers are used to separate clearly the rare item from the standard library materials flow. These cases are usually locked at the sending library and can be unlocked only at the receiving library. Special paperwork that tracks exactly when and how these materials move is usually maintained. Typically these shipments make up a tiny fraction of a courier delivery volume. The limited demand allows the extra precautions to be implemented at low cost to the courier service.

Other Delivery Services

Other delivery services are being considered or developed by courier managers around the country, including a few that bring value added or even financial remuneration to the delivery service:

> Deliveries to computer and equipment repair places are relatively common and are of great value to participating libraries that need to ship bulky equipment.

Libraries are charging for home delivery. If patrons are willing to pay postage and handling to have library materials delivered via the USPS to their home with a stamped return envelope, why shouldn't the library provide the service? Why can't the delivery service run a specialized van for home delivery—again, billing patrons on the basis of recovery expenses with administrative overhead. (Free access to home delivery for patrons is discussed in chapter 11.)

Libraries are developing arrangements with book resellers. These companies offer a part of the resale value of library discards back to the participating libraries. A library courier service can recoup some of the cost of the delivery service by assisting in shipping to resellers. The next step is for the library delivery service to become a reseller itself. The Colorado Library Consortium is currently running a pilot of such a project.

Some patrons need special equipment to access library collections. The courier service could deliver this material. This can be done in a partnership with another nonprofit organization that provides such equipment to people with special needs.

Perhaps a courier service could connect with library vendors such as book binders, new book shippers, and supply companies. A courier located near a shipping facility for a library book supplier like Baker and Taylor or Yankee Books or a book binder like Houchen Bindery could find a way to speed delivery of ordered materials to libraries while raising operating capital.

The more libraries study the world of supply chain management, the more we can learn about opportunities for providing better services to our library patrons while possibly recuperating some operating capital. This topic is a relatively new concept among physical delivery managers, but one likely to see growth in the coming years.

Note

1. See Peter Hernon and Ellen Altman, *Assessing Service Quality: Satisfying the Expectations of Library Customers* (Chicago: American Library Association, 1998).

Part Four

The Future of
Physical Delivery

11

Home Delivery

Lori Ayre and Jim Myers

Home delivery is not new to libraries. Specialized homebound delivery services, bookmobiles, deliveries to nursing homes, and other similar services have been around for some time. Academic libraries have been delivering to distance education students for many years. A few public library systems, such as Orange County in Florida and Topeka and Shawnee County in Kansas, have figured out how to provide direct home delivery to their patrons and have done so for years. But home delivery has not become the norm in public libraries as was predicted in a 1970 by Robert Jordan in *Tomorrow's Library.*[1]

In this chapter we look at how patron expectations have changed as a result of social networking and Internet shopping, and how patrons are now driving the demand for home delivery. Patrons are saying, "Well, if Netflix and Amazon can deliver, why can't the library?" And the answer is that libraries *can* deliver to the home, economically. We also offer details about Orange County's successful home delivery service. Home delivery is no more expensive than maintaining a mid-sized branch library and is routinely evaluated by patrons as the library's best service. The only things stopping home delivery from becoming a norm across the country are the perception that it is too expensive and a lack of knowledge among librarians about how to manage such a service.

HOME DELIVERY: THE FULFILLMENT MODEL

Have you ever wanted something, gone out to the store to get it, but found the store did not have your item in or know when it would become available? When that happened, what action did you take? Did you choose to wait for it, or did you try another store? Let's assume you decided to wait for it and you put your name on a waiting list, even though you have no idea when the item will come in. Now imagine, the store calls you and says it is in and you should come get it right away. In fact, if you don't come and get it within seven days, the store will sell the item to someone else. I think we could all agree that this store would not get the highest marks in customer service.

Yet this is how the current system of holds works at most public libraries and, though holds are popular, theirs is not a very good service model. It leaves the customer in limbo, not knowing when an item will be available. And it expects the customer to do too much of the work involved in getting the desired item.

It is time to treat library users more like the valued customers they are and to acknowledge that their time is scarce and valuable. Adding the option to home-deliver holds, instead of relying on the "come and get it" model, is one way to extend the fulfillment options available to library users. Other fulfillment options that should be considered include direct delivery, such as special delivery to any specified address, personal delivery, expedited delivery, and e-delivery.

Libraries do not offer direct delivery of holds for several reasons: it is expensive, it is labor intensive, and it could result in keeping items out of circulation longer (when shipping time is accounted for). Some say that library customers enjoy coming to the library and would not *want* to have material delivered to them, or that library users are less likely to return material received via mail. Another drawback is that today's ILSs are not designed to support home delivery.

There are also many reasons to offer direct delivery of library material to our customer's home or office or vacation getaway. As twenty-first-century consumers, we don't wait for things. We are more likely to choose something "good enough" rather than wait for what we really want. In most cases, there is almost always another choice that will result in our immediate satisfaction. For example, there are many ways to get information—books, music, movies. Libraries are just one option among many.

Today's library users, like everyone, expect fast and efficient service. They expect to be able to find what they want. They expect to be able to get it when and where they want it. They do not expect to wait and wonder when an item they have requested will be available. They do not expect to do a lot of work to get items they have "ordered." Understandably, they expect libraries to operate like most twenty-first-century businesses.

Libraries began allowing customers to place holds on items several years ago. They began doing the work of bringing material to the customer's nearby library branch rather than expecting the customer to travel to another branch to get it. Library users loved the service, and the number of holds skyrocketed. Libraries then began allowing customers to pick up holds and return material at any branch. Again, customers responded with enthusiasm. They loved the convenience of the service.

Libraries soon began to suffer from the burden of their own success. Material transfers between libraries overwhelmed library circulation staff as they tried to keep up with all the holds that needed to be pulled, routed to the right location, and prepared for the hold shelves. Shelving units of browsing material were converted to hold shelves and interlibrary delivery volume doubled and tripled as these popular services were rolled out.

Convenience Trumps Everything

The primary reason library users prefer to place holds and pick up and drop off material at the library branch of their choice is convenience. Customer convenience is more important than speed, privacy, and sometimes money. Convenience trumps everything.

People generally have either time or money but not both. A 2006 ALA study found that 90 percent of library users taking out books had incomes between $15,000 and $35,000.[2] These people do not have a lot of money. They are using the library because the material is free. Even if they have to wait to get what they want, they will. They do not complain too much if they have to wait for weeks or even months to get a popular DVD. They do not complain that they have to come to the library (possibly at some cost and possibly great inconvenience) to pick up their requested material—because it is free, and that's critical. Despite the inconvenience, some customers accept the "cost" of doing business at the library.

What about the people in higher income brackets; where are they getting their books and DVDs? These are the Amazon.com and Netflix users whose time is more precious than their money. In many cases, these people would like to support the library, but they cannot afford to wait for items to find their way to a library branch. These users prefer to purchase the book (new or used) and have it delivered to their home or office. For them, it is preferable to pay for the book and the shipment in exchange for the convenience of getting the item delivered and knowing when it will arrive. Amazon.com customers do not have to leave home to get what they want, and they know exactly when their material will arrive. Many used book stores are offering the same convenient online services, and the material can be purchased very inexpensively.

Netflix relies on the same appeal to convenience and takes the service one step further. Not only does the item arrive in the customer's mailbox, but it can be returned the same way. Further, the customer can queue up several requests and not have to bother requesting items one by one. They just magically arrive. Watch one movie, return it, and here comes another one from the wish list. What could be more convenient than that?

Broaden the Base of Library Users

According to the aforementioned ALA study, 63 percent of Americans owned a library card in 2006. The same study reported that 25 percent of people with a library card had not visited the library in the past year. In other words, everyone loves the library—in theory. They want to support libraries. They take pride in having a library card. But most of these library supporters do not actually use the library. Perhaps it just is not convenient enough.

It is time to develop a service commitment that works for most people, a service model that respects every customer's time and makes the library an easier choice for everyone to make. Ultimately, by providing high-quality, convenient services, our libraries can build a stronger base of support and bring in more funding. As long as libraries are seen as a public good but one that higher-income users do not use, they run the risk of losing the support of those higher-income users. Expanding library services to include fee-based (if necessary), convenience-oriented services will address some of the needs of a category of users who currently do not use the library.

Turnaround Time Matters

Although convenience is the holy grail of customer service, turnaround time matters too. Our concept of an "acceptable wait time" continues to shorten. Before word processing and fax machines, wait time was measured in days. Today we think in minutes, not days and certainly not weeks. Many baby boomers use e-mail every day and expect responses to their messages the same day. People in their twenties do not use e-mail because it is not instantaneous enough. They operate in Instant Message increments.

The younger you are, the shorter your acceptable wait time. Kids today are unfamiliar with concepts like photo finishing, where you have to wait to see your photos. They can watch a TV show any time because they have pay-per-view or TIVO (a popular brand of digital video recorder). As these young people grow up, the slow turnaround times considered acceptable in libraries will no longer be acceptable. This generation of library users will not care about the intricacies of ILL and the effort made to get the item they have requested—they just want the result. Already, books and other library material are commodities. Libraries are not the keepers of a scarce number of tomes. Libraries are just one option for getting an item that is readily available from any number of places. So, if the turnaround time does not fit the need, users will go elsewhere.

It Will Only Get Worse from Here

Users value convenience and expect fast turnaround times. They also expect everything to be readily findable. Researchers' experience with search engines is that they can always find an acceptable answer. They can identify a decent restaurant, learn about possible vacation destinations, get answers to simple questions, or find an essay or blog post or podcast on any topic of interest. Increasingly, search engines are also helping them find books and other library materials. Libraries are benefiting from the work of OCLC to make library material discoverable through search engines like Google and Yahoo. Google and Yahoo users can simply install a plug-in that allows them to use their regular search engine to search all the holdings in OCLC's WorldCat for library material. From the WorldCat interface, they can then borrow it from their own library or order it from Amazon.com.

The ability to discover more easily the material available in libraries everywhere will create yet more demand. What OCLC has done with WorldCat is take advantage of the network effects of aggregating the supply of all library material (that is represented in WorldCat), thereby expanding the number of potential users. As more users discover library material using their preferred search tools (vs. the library catalog), more requests will be made for interlibrary transfers and loans.

Library users appreciate and value the convenience of placing their own hold requests and being able to choose where to pick up and drop off library material. All libraries providing these services are struggling with the delivery challenges associated with moving material from branch to branch and library to library. Sending out material from a library directly to the library user solves many problems for the library and creates an even more convenient service for the user.

Direct Delivery Reduces Delivery Volume

To fill user requests, most libraries pick items off the shelf, scan them to put them into transit, and prepare the material for their courier. Their courier picks up the requested material and the receiving library has to scan each item to trigger the hold, prepare the material for the holds shelf (label it with the customer's name), and then put it on the holds shelf. When the item is returned by the customer, it must again be scanned to determine where it belongs and possibly be put into transit again.

For the customer, the transaction requires two trips to the library. For the library, it requires several scans of the bar code and up to two trips via courier and the requisite label printing for putting the item on the hold shelf and routing the material from library to library. That's a lot of overhead. In addition, the customer placing the hold may not know when her held item will be available and may not even want it by the time it hits the hold shelf. Libraries report that 10–20 percent of holds are never picked up. Most libraries allow a week or even ten days for holds to be picked up (and this does not include the circulation period), so requested items that do not get picked up also do not circulate or fill pending requests for over a week.

If libraries shipped items directly to the customer, the transaction would eliminate at least two and possibly as many as four trips between locations (two library-to-library trips and two patron trips to the library) and would ensure that library material was circulating with customers instead of sitting on shelves or in vans. If the library used USPS Media Mail, the item would arrive at the customer's home within a day or two and the cost to the library would be less than $2.00.

Ideally, the library could offer a range of choices to library customers. The Topeka and Shawnee County Public Library mails all hold requests by default, but customers who prefer to pick up their material can simply enter their phone number in the comment box and be notified when the item is ready for them.

Availability of Delivery Options Would Bring in New Library Users

Local businesses might be more inclined to use library resources if they could get material as quickly as they need it. Law firms, medical offices, and other businesses pay personal messengers to deliver documents every day. If direct delivery services were available, they would be more inclined to use the library as a resource for articles, books, and other research material. But waiting for the slow wheels of ILL to turn does not work well for today's businesses. Business customers and higher-income customers are among those who would be more likely to use the library if it offered a service model that made sense for their lives, even if it cost them more money.

Although some people do not use the library because it is inconvenient for them, some "digital natives," people who grow up comfortable with technology, are making extraordinary use of the library without ever entering the building. Downloadable audio books and e-books are popular with users who have not used the library before. Online databases, digital repositories, digital libraries, and other online services have created this new category of library users, whose home branch is the e-branch. These users would be more inclined to use nonelectronic library materials such as books and DVDs if they could browse, discover, download, or request these items online too.

Even for those library customers with more time and less money, home delivery may provide cost savings in certain situations. For example, if a customer has to pay $2.00 to ride a bus to the library, it may make more economic sense to pay for having the item mailed to their home.

Direct Delivery Leverages Library Spaces

According to William Sannwald, the author of *Checklist of Library Building Design Considerations,* the current cost of building a library is $400 per square foot (fully loaded building cost).[3] Libraries report their success in terms of total number of circulations (total number of check-outs) and collection turnover (total number of check-outs divided by holdings). The more time library material spends on book carts, in transit, and on hold shelves, the less that material can circulate and the greater the cost of storing that item.

Unless a library was built in the past few years, it is likely to have too little space for current demands. Library users want more from their library space than rows of books and quiet study areas. They still expect room to read quietly, but they also want spaces for the kids to interact and play games, plenty of public access computers, meeting rooms, cafes, display areas for browsing current popular titles, and quick and easy-to-use self-service options for checking in, getting one's holds, and checking out. Older library spaces cannot effectively accommodate these mounting needs.

Reducing the space dedicated to hold shelves by offering direct delivery is one way to expand a service that customers value while getting back some of the library space in-library customers appreciate. Instead of filling public spaces with hold shelves and extra self-check machines to accommodate those people who just want to get in and out, enable those customers to receive and return their material via direct delivery. The shipping process happens in staff work areas or, even better, at central library fulfillment centers, where a collection of material is stored in high-density file systems and is specifically targeted to the e-branch users, eliminating the need for branch-to-branch transfers and freeing up valuable public areas.

WHAT IT TAKES TO ROLL OUT DIRECT DELIVERY SERVICE

Providing direct delivery service involves the following components: an appropriate software interface, packaging, and a courier or shipper. It may also require a change in attitude about what constitutes a library user.

Software Interface

The biggest hurdle for today's library is the software interface. None of the currently available library systems provide a direct delivery module designed to support a high volume of material. Many library systems provide a patron module that tracks items shipped to individuals who qualify as "homebound." But when offering direct delivery as an option for everyone, libraries need to be able to generate shipping labels with bar codes, choose between delivery services, and offer the customer control over how to use (and possibly pay for) the service. To take advantage of special rates and special services (address verification, Saturday shipment, next-day service, second-day service, tracking, etc.), the library must output patron data to third-party shipping software (e.g., Endicia, United States Postal Service Shipping Assistant, Dydacomp Mail Order Manager) or integrate these features into an existing ILS module. Fortunately, the new open-source library system products are much more conducive to this type of integration, but it is not supported by many of today's non-open-source ILS vendors. As a result, it is more labor intensive than necessary to ship items via the USPS or other commercial shipping vendors.

The software should be easy for library customers to use too. Customers must be able to set up direct delivery as the default choice or request direct delivery on an item-by-item basis. Customers must be able to verify the shipping address, authorize payment (if applicable), and cancel direct delivery requests that have not been filled. At this time, these features are not part of any of the software interfaces available from ILS vendors.

Packaging

Packaging can become an impediment for libraries that would like to offer home delivery. The packaging requirement depends on the material being shipped, the vendor being used, and the way the item will be returned to the library. The Orange County (Florida) library system uses basic jiffy bags with simple address labels printed by its ILS. It has been able to minimize the work associated with packaging because it delivers material via a contracted courier service. All the sorting is done manually by the couriers. A library that wishes to automate the sorting of material needs to be able to sort material automatically, and this generally requires a bar code. Libraries using automation or outsourcing the shipping to a commercial shipper may be better off using the shipping contractor's labels, envelopes, and boxes.

Ideally, packaging is streamlined with as few variations as possible. For example, perhaps the library offers two levels of service, such as next-day or Media Mail. These choices depend on the library's goals. If the goal is to cover the cost of shipping by using a low-cost delivery service, USPS Media Mail may be the best bet. If the goal is to get the material to the user as quickly as possible, USPS First Class mail or next-day UPS or FedEx may work better. Some libraries may attempt to meet both goals: provide a free, low-cost service and a fee-based expedited service. Ideally, libraries offering more choices will find a fulfillment center that can prepare and package material as needed. If libraries are packaging and shipping out of their own facilities, it is important that they keep the necessary supplies to a minimum and avoid using tape and staples (which increase the handling requirements) as much as possible.

Courier or Shipper?

Most libraries use UPS or FedEx for sending and receiving ILL material between library systems and a courier service for deliveries within a library system. These two provider types are good choices for those applications. But for direct delivery to library customers, neither the local courier nor UPS or FedEx are a good fit. Couriers do not have the ability to add new locations to their route and still stay on their 24-hour turnaround schedule. UPS and FedEx are not a good fit because of the high cost of single-item, short-distance deliveries. Although UPS and FedEx may offer competitive pricing with the USPS when it comes to larger volumes or longer distances, the USPS is ideal for delivering small packages to lots of nearby locations. The USPS delivers to everyone in a library's service area every day, and its specialty is very small packages (e.g., letters, magazines). For this reason, it can offer better pricing for the service than UPS and FedEx. To the extent that a library can bundle items destined for the same zip code, the pricing becomes very attractive. Although it is unlikely that the cost for direct or home delivery will ever compare to the per-item cost of a scheduled courier service (generally under fifty cents), it can be kept under $2.00 per item on single shipments and possibly less (per item) when several items are shipped at once.

THE FUTURE OF DIRECT DELIVERY

One of the biggest hurdles to offering direct delivery as a service option is the perspective that, if the customer does not come into the library, then his or her use of the library does not count the same as one who does. Although there are many good reasons for customers to come to the library, many of those reasons do not apply to some people. For example, the great children's programs offered at libraries are not a draw for working adults with no children, but they may enjoy getting DVDs or CDs to use on their own home theater system. Quiet, public reading places may not be a draw for someone who commutes four hours a day to work, but that same person would appreciate the steady supply of audiobooks available from the library.

Some libraries are starting to recognize the importance of the e-branch user and offering e-cards—a virtual library card that verifies the customer's address but does not require a driver's license or other physical form of identification. E-cards can be used however the library chooses; most libraries limit e-cardholders to electronic resources until the e-card is converted to a full library card.

Like e-card users, direct delivery customers may be another untapped pool of library users with unique needs: they want to use physical library material but do not want to come to the library. Many libraries refuse to offer fee-based services, believing that they create a two-tiered system of users. But by not providing services that are convenient enough for the lifestyles of many potential customers, the library is choosing not to address their needs. Is a two-tiered system worse than ignoring the needs of a whole category of potential library users?

Some potential users may support the library and see that it fills a public service, but they do not necessarily see the library as relevant to their lives. It would be nice if people with more disposable income, or no children, or jobs that involve very long commutes also benefited from library services. Why not give these users even more reasons to vote for those library bonds.

Home delivery has proved to be a popular service for every library that has offered it for free. Orange County citizens report that the home delivery service is one of the most valued services the library provides. The library offers the service for free, arguing that the cost of the service is comparable (actually cheaper) than operating another library outlet.

There is no doubt that free direct delivery would be popular with every community, but if the library cannot offer the service for free, why not consider charging a small fee for the service? Direct delivery offers a way to meet some of the needs of potential customers (and voters) currently underserved by the library. For libraries that decide to offer fee-based or convenience-based services, it is important to ensure that paying the fee is as convenient as the service itself. Therefore, libraries may need to find ways to debit the user's library account, credit card, or PayPal account automatically. For libraries that choose to offer direct delivery for free, it will likely be necessary to limit the number of items that can be sent out within a given period so that customers do not overwhelm the system.

One of the changes happening in libraries today is automation replacing manual systems for moving and sorting material as well as some circulation functions. This trend began with automated self check-out systems, and we can see the continuing trend with automated self check-in systems. With automated check-in, the material is checked in and removed from the cardholder's account and then sorted to a tote or trolley for shelving or additional processing.

Automated check-in, check-out, and sorting are done much more easily and with fewer errors using an RFID-based system. RFID tags can also be used to store information the library system writes to the tag. Whereas first-generation RFID tags are being used as glorified (and very expensive) bar codes, next-generation tags will be used to aid in materials handling and ILL processing. For example, in a few years, it will likely be common for information about holds and pickup locations to be written to the library material's RFID tag so the item can be more easily found on the shelf and routed to the desired location. Standards for what to write on the library RFID tags are still being developed. These standards will also ensure that customer privacy is protected so that the tags can be used to store information beyond a simple bar code.

As library sorters become more common (and library spaces are designed to accommodate larger sorters), library material will be automatically sorted not just to trolleys or carts for reshelving and totes for delivery but also to destinations that support other delivery mechanisms. For example, sorters can be equipped with discharge locations for "direct ship" items presorted by destination zip code so that staff can easily bundle groups of ten items to take advantage of USPS bundle rate pricing. Printers can be configured to print out the right labels (e.g., routing labels for couriers, USPS Media Mail labels for direct delivery) automatically to match the items' delivery mechanism. There are many unexploited avenues available to libraries that are committed to offering direct delivery.

It is worth noting that another way to implement direct delivery is scan-on-demand. With the new high-powered scanners, it will soon be practical for libraries to digitize library material and e-mail it to their library customers, or perhaps make it available online. As demand for electronic versions of material grows, this will be an important delivery option to provide customers as well.

Much of the technology needed to support direct delivery approaches (e.g., direct delivery and scan-on-demand) is expensive and requires a fair amount of space. More and more libraries should be thinking about creating service centers that optimize the library's ability to fill these orders. These service or fulfillment centers can be used to sort material for the library system (or consortium) and to separate out items for direct delivery or perhaps e-delivery processing. It is not practical for individual libraries to own scan-on-demand equipment or to install high-volume, high-speed sorters. This approach does, however, begin to make sense for larger library systems or library consortia that can distribute the cost of the equipment among several libraries.

Using large warehouse spaces for materials handling functions is cheaper for the library system than using up valuable public areas and staff areas at each of the libraries. As libraries grapple with increasing volumes of material being circulated and moved around their library system, we will see more and more library systems establishing service centers to support materials handling and request fulfillment.

HOME DELIVERY AT THE ORANGE COUNTY LIBRARY SYSTEM

The Orange County Library System (OCLS) serves a community of 1.3 million people across a thousand square miles in central Florida. Founded in 1923 as the Albertson Public Library in downtown Orlando, today OCLS includes the Orlando Public Library (main library) and fourteen branch locations throughout the county. The OCLS service area is all of Orange County with the exception of two municipalities. The population is diverse and spread evenly across age groups. OCLS maintains a circulating collection of 1.5 million items and has more than 450,000 registered borrowers. In fiscal year 2007, the system circulated

9.3 million items. Approximately 8 percent of those circulated items were delivered to patrons via the popular home delivery service—MAYL (Materials Access from Your Library).

Over the past several years, OCLS has emphasized providing a variety of programs, computer classes, and technology-focused products. Positive attendance figures and digital statistics show that these products and services are well received. But it is MAYL, now in its fourth decade of operation, that consistently rates as the library system's most popular service according to patron surveys.

History of MAYL

OCLS initiated its home delivery service in 1974. In the early 1970s, as the impact of Disney World began to transform central Florida into a major tourist destination, the library system consisted of the main library, nine small branches, and an aging bookmobile. The population of Orange County was 350,000. As development stretched in all directions, OCLS director Glenn Miller wanted to replace the bookmobile and still provide meaningful library service to residents throughout the entire service area. A books-by-mail service was the answer, connecting people to the library by bringing the library to them. Resident cardholders could call and request titles, and the library would mail the books to their homes at no cost to the patrons. OCLS would devote resources to provide the service just as it provided resources for branches. Home delivery was the library-without-walls.

In 1975, the first full year of the service, 9,000 books were mailed to patrons. Growth was slow but steady throughout the remainder of the decade. In the 1980s, as the main library was expanded to three times its original size and the network of branches began to reach more distant communities around Orange County, home delivery started to emerge as one of the library's most popular services. Processing the requests for home delivery became the responsibility of the Special Services department. The requests were maintained on handwritten cards that doubled as mailing labels, a process that continued for the first twenty-two years of the service. Known simply as Books-by-Mail through these formative years, the home delivery service was dubbed MAYL in the late 1980s. The acronym originally stood for Mailbox Access to Your Library. By 1990, volume was averaging 18,000 books per month.

Though OCLS possessed an AV collection throughout the home delivery era, it was not until 1990 that AV materials were made eligible for request. By 1992, 10 percent of MAYL volume was AV material. Overall growth accelerated through the early 1990s. Monthly circulation was 23,000 in 1994 when the system faced a new dilemma. The USPS announced a 70 percent postage increase for library book rate. In June 1994, the *Orlando Sentinel* ran a story about MAYL and the impending postal increase, reporting on the library's search for home delivery alternatives.

After reading the *Orlando Sentinel* article, friends Rick Bennett and Dennis Clay created a proposal for OCLS. Bennett had worked for FedEx and Clay for the USPS. They were confident they could start a company to provide the library with quick delivery, at a competitive cost, with less-intensive package preparation for library staff. In his letter to OCLS, Bennett wrote, "You do have an alternative. One that I feel could be mutually beneficial for all involved."

In early 1995, the library began a trial run with Bennett and Clay's fledgling operation, Priority Express Parcel (PEP). Initially delivering to a few selected zip codes, PEP quickly demonstrated a high level of reliability and efficiency. Charging $1.35 per package regardless of weight, PEP offered a rate slightly less than the average USPS Library Book rate. But along with that favorable rate, PEP delivered packages within two days. USPS delivery typically took (and still takes) up to seven days. The small roster of PEP drivers proved to be dependable and courteous, and the company was soon delivering requested items to homes throughout most of the OCLS service region. MAYL became Materials Access from Your Library, the word "mailbox" conspicuously dropped.

By 2000, PEP had ten employees and was delivering 88 percent of requested OCLS items. That same year, OCLS began outsourcing interlocation delivery to PEP, another alternative that continues to be mutually beneficial nearly a decade later. Today PEP delivers 92 percent of OCLS requests (the remaining 8 percent are delivered via USPS or picked up by patrons). Package cost has increased fifty cents, to $1.85, in the thirteen years PEP has delivered MAYL for OCLS, a rate that still compares favorably to the current average USPS Media Mail rate. To keep up with the prolific growth of MAYL over the past decade, PEP has doubled the size of its staff. Most deliveries are still made within two days, and none take longer than three days.

MAYL volume has risen tremendously over the past ten years. The OCLS website was introduced in May 1998, and that year 2,500 requests were made by patrons via the Web. In May 1999, the number was 8,500. By 2002, 17,000 requests monthly were originating from the website, representing 50 percent of requests systemwide. In May 2008, 69,000 holds were placed online, 85 percent of all requests.

Clearly, MAYL is perfectly suited for the online world, almost as if it was conceived all those years ago with the digital age in mind. The service initiated by the library during the nation's first gas crisis now helps OCLS stay relevant during the nation's most recent energy crisis. The library-without-walls first envisioned in the 1970s has become the system's third-highest circulating agency, checking out 720,791 requested items in 2007. In 2008, MAYL circulation neared 800,000 items.

From Request to Package

The MAYL process has always been about making adjustments. From learning to operate postage machines and sort canvas mail sacks to negotiating three computer system migrations in less than two decades, library staff working with home delivery have had to manage significant change and accommodate substantial growth.

Today, OCLS uses a paging list process to locate requested material that should be on the shelf. Staff use these location-specific lists daily to search for the requested items and send found copies to Special Services for processing. If all owned copies of a requested title are checked out, staff are prompted to send the item to Special Services during the check-in process. The main library's daily regular paging list is typically 500–700 items, with 150–250 lease books and DVDs appearing on the daily floating list. For branches, regular paging lists fall in the 75–200 item range, and floating lists are anywhere between 25 and 100 items. Today, 60 percent of OCLS requests are for books, 20 percent for DVDs, 10 percent for music CDs, and 5 percent for CD books.

Special Services received its name many years ago, back when, in addition to Books-by-Mail, the department also handled ILL and talking books. The focus became exclusive to processing MAYL material in the early 1990s. The Special Services staff currently consists of one full-time manager, one full-time coordinator, eleven full-time clerks, and six part-time clerks. The department occupies a 10,000-square-foot portion of the basement floor in the main library, a space large enough to conduct all MAYL activity and store all related supplies.

Chief among department supplies are the padded mailers used to ship requested material; four different sizes accommodate all types of items. Patrons are encouraged to return the mailers for reuse; the mailers have "Reusable—Please Return" printed on one side. Approximately 80 percent of requests are sent out in mailers that were previously used. Whenever possible, multiple items requested by a patron are placed together in one padded mailer. When staff begin to recognize a particular patron as a heavy user of MAYL, a note is placed on the patron's account that directs everyone in the department to set aside that patron's items until the end of the day. All items for the patron are then packaged together.

With 92 percent of MAYL items being delivered by PEP, sorting packages for distribution mostly means placing them in one of several large bins wheeled in and out by PEP drivers throughout the day. About 4 percent of MAYL patrons still receive material through the postal service; this is usually because the mailing address is a P.O. box or the patron's residential address is too remote for inclusion in PEP's delivery area. Special Services has its own postage machine in the department. Staff post 100–150 packages a day and place them in a postal wire sent out the following morning. The remaining 4 percent of packages are picked up by patrons at an established OCLS location. This is typically arranged at the request of the patron, but a small number of pickup arrangements are initiated by the library after patrons report two or more failures to receive delivered packages. Items for pickup at the main library are delivered by Special Services to hold desks within the building. PEP gathers the packages being picked up at branch locations to be included in the following day's interlocation delivery.

From Dock to Door

PEP headquarters is two miles from the main library. Most of the building, approximately 650 square feet, is devoted to sorting. The fenced-in parking lot provides space for the fleet of vehicles, sixteen small pickup trucks with toppers and two 18-foot box trucks. MAYL packages are delivered by couriers using the pickup trucks, and interlocation delivery is divided by two drivers using the box trucks. Each courier drives about 100 miles a day. Combined, they make approximately two thousand stops daily, using an average of 100 gallons of gas. The delivery drivers stop at thirteen of the fourteen branches six days a week; the fourteenth branch receives delivery via a courier delivering MAYL packages in its neighborhood. Together, the interlocation delivery routes cover 175 miles each day.

Including Bennett and Clay, PEP employs twenty people. All PEP staff members wear company shirts (polo style or T-shirt with logo) and black shorts or pants. Additional uniform items provided include baseball hats and jackets. Staff are salaried, which allows for individual scheduling flexibility and promotes a sense of ownership of the routes for drivers. Health insurance is provided for employees. PEP suffers little turnover; most of the staff have been with the company more than five years.

The interlocation drivers begin their routes at 8:00 a.m. One driver delivers to six branches north of the main library. The other driver delivers to seven branches to the south. Along with returning items owned by the main library to the shelving staff and turning over interoffice mail to the mailroom, the drivers deliver requested material found at branches to Special Services.

The MAYL package-sorting area at the PEP warehouse is a large rectangular room. All along the perimeter, fifteen built-in wooden sections, approximately 3 feet deep, represent each of the courier routes. Throughout the day, full bins are wheeled into the center of the room, and packages are sorted into the appropriate sections by the employee stationed at the warehouse and any driver who happens to be there at the time. After completing their deliveries for the day and returning to the warehouse, the couriers further sort the packages in their sections and prepare their routes for the next workday.

All routes are split in half and completed over two-day periods. The couriers alternate between one side of the route and the other from day to day, resulting in the great majority of items reaching the address within two days of being checked out in Special Services. Couriers set their own daily schedule, the only rule being that deliveries not be made in the dark.

The couriers are instructed to observe the elements when making deliveries. PEP provides reusable plastic bags to protect the packages. Depending on weather conditions and the amount of shelter provided at the door of the residence, couriers decide whether or not to use a bag. For deliveries to gated communities, Special Services staff contacts patrons to obtain gate codes that are passed along to the couriers. Driveways are avoided, unless there is no safe place to park on the road. When delivering to a fenced residence, the courier puts the package in a bag and twists it shut on the gate. By contacting the library or calling PEP directly (the company lists its phone number on the bags), some patrons give specific instructions for the delivery of packages. These instructions are printed with the address on the mailing label, prompting couriers to place packages in containers near doors, to leave them at leasing offices, to always knock when delivering, or to follow any number of other directives.

It is not officially part of PEP's service to deliver material from MAYL patrons back to the library. However, when making a delivery, couriers will accept library items and padded mailers presented by patrons and deliver the material to Special Services the following day. This courtesy reflects the company's commitment to customer service. Bennett and Clay long ago established the understanding at PEP that each employee serves as an ambassador for the library, and that philosophy is exemplified each day by the PEP staff.

Cost Comparison and Return on Investment

One undeniable truth about MAYL is that an increase in delivery volume means an increase in the overall cost of the service. The enormous growth of MAYL over the past ten years is seen not only in circulation figures but also in the OCLS budget. Including Special Services staff salaries and benefits, MAYL operations costs in 2008 were projected to be $1,867,000. This represented 4.4 percent of the library's anticipated budget expenditures, up from 2.9 percent in 1998. Cost of delivery in 2008 was projected to account for 3.1 percent of anticipated expenditures.

Despite the inevitable increase in overall cost that comes with the service's rise in popularity, a cost-per-unit comparison of MAYL with the costs of OCLS physical locations indicates that the service is one of the library's most cost-effective operations. Dividing the overall cost of the service by the volume of checked-out requests shows that each MAYL transaction costs $2.46. This figure has increased only nine cents over the past ten years. Only four of the library's fifteen locations have a lower cost per checked-out item.

To appreciate the value of MAYL fully, it is important to consider other factors that help measure the return on investment for both the individual taxpayer and the community as a whole. For the individual, there is the obvious savings in time, gas, and other associated driving costs. The convenience offered by MAYL cannot be underestimated. The service makes it possible for someone new to experience the library in a tangible way without leaving home.

From the library website, Orange County residents can register for a library card. If the registration process is successful, patrons receive their library cards in the mail within ten days. They can then request items from the online catalog, and the MAYL service puts the material in their hands without them ever actually visiting a location. Though OCLS is proud of its locations and provides a great variety of programs and services to draw visitors, there is also the recognition that a significant portion of customers prefer to use the library virtually. A 2005 online survey about MAYL, taken by 1,600 patrons, revealed that 33 percent utilized the library exclusively through the website and home delivery.

The individual also gains from the benefits MAYL provides to the community at large. Just as the service was ahead of its time by being so well suited for the Internet, MAYL was also a green service before anyone knew what that meant. Simply put, home delivery helps keep cars off the road, which in turn lowers fuel emissions and reduces wear and tear on roads that the taxpayers help maintain.

To illustrate these benefits more specifically, current Special Services head Jo Ann Sampson recently used statistics provided by Bennett and Clay to measure the service's positive environmental (and economical) impact on the community. Consider the two thousand deliveries the fleet of PEP couriers make each day, and the 100 gallons of gas required to make those deliveries. Then imagine residents from those two thousand households getting in their vehicles and driving to the library to pick up requested items. Allowing for a five-mile round-trip, these patrons will drive a combined 10,000 miles. The U.S. government reports that the average mileage for today's vehicles is 23 miles per gallon. Using that average, the 10,000 miles traveled by patrons picking up requested material would use 435 gallons of gas. In other words, the two thousand deliveries made by PEP take less than 25 percent of the fuel it would take for patrons to pick up the material from the library. At $3.50 per gallon, PEP spends $350 daily. The cost for patrons would exceed $1,500. Spread that out over a year (260 workdays), and you see a difference of $299,000.

Dare to Be Relevant: Embracing Home Delivery

Back in 1974 when OCLS started the home delivery service, the vision was clear. Books-by-Mail was a way to replace an old bookmobile, a way to reach distant sections of the library service area that might not have a nearby branch. But it was also about rethinking the traditional process of filling requests for patrons, and about redefining what it meant to provide good library service. Traditionally, the patron made a request for a title, the library eventually secured the title for the patron, and then the patron had to take action to collect the item. One of the central values intrinsic to MAYL is that it takes the onus off patrons to do anything else once they request a title. The responsibility of completing the transaction is built into the process. If this was forward thinking in the 1970s, it is paramount to remaining relevant today. Consumers have become increasingly accustomed to services that cater to their schedules and make convenience a top priority. As public libraries continue to examine their ever-changing role in the lives of their residents, it is important that they recognize models such as Amazon.com and Netflix as the standard against which they are measured.

To initiate a home delivery service, a library must be willing to overlook apparent obstacles. The logistics of carrying out the service can be considerable, but they are certainly manageable with proper planning and research. The most significant hurdle is the perception of cost. When discussing home delivery as an option, most objections are based on the sense that the service is a luxury. There is a common misconception that a home delivery transaction costs more than one taking place in a physical location. However, as illustrated by our MAYL cost-per-unit comparison, that simply is not the case. The organization must consider the cost of operating the physical branch, including overhead, building maintenance, and development and sustenance of the collection. By contrast, a home delivery operation may be housed within an existing location, and the collection, whether for a single-location library or for a system or consortium, is already in place. Instead of facility and collection costs, the home delivery service expenditures are directed toward delivery costs. It goes without saying that the commitment of leadership within the organization is vital to the success of a home delivery service. Understanding the true cost by transaction of the service and weighing that cost versus patron satisfaction will prove to be valuable tools for the library's administration when questioned about the viability of home delivery.

OTHER HOME DELIVERY MODELS

Challenges to home delivery's viability are likely. But it is also quite likely that patron support for the service will be strong and vocal. Two public library models of home delivery besides MAYL—one a recent operation in a neighboring central Florida county, the other a twenty-year veteran of home delivery in the country's heartland—both report tremendous customer satisfaction.

The Topeka and Shawnee County Public Library (TSCPL), Kansas, has been operating a home delivery service since the mid-1980s. Paul Brennan, collections manager for TSCPL, oversees the service. Brennan indicates that the origin of the service can be traced to a cost/benefit analysis conducted by TSCPL administrators about adding parking for the library. Instead of constructing a parking garage, TSCPL decided to initiate a home delivery service. TSCPL's home delivery of requested items is free to all cardholders, and material is sent through USPS using library book rate. All circulating material in the collection is eligible for home delivery. The service is extremely popular with TSCPL patrons and, reports Brennan, "pretty central to what we do. There is complete buy-in to the service from the top of the organization." Brennan believes the service reaches people in the county that otherwise would not use the library. Critical questions about the service are few, but typically they center on the cost the library incurs by offering the service. Like OCLS, TSCPL can point to cost-per-unit statistics to illustrate the value of the service.

In 2007, TSCPL mailed 153,438 items to customers, representing 4.2 percent of the library's total circulation. Provided the title is available, it takes two to three days for a requested item to be checked out for the patron, and two to three more days for it to be mailed. Two full-time staff members focus on processing the requests once the item is checked out to the patron. Patrons are responsible for the return of material, either by paying return postage or returning the items to the library or to one of the drop boxes located throughout the county.

Polk County, Florida, is southwest of Orange County and has approximately 560,000 residents spread across more than 2,000 square miles. The Polk County Library Cooperative (PCLC) began a home delivery service called B-Mail in 2006. Material requested through B-Mail is mailed via USPS library book rate. Though 75 percent of PCLC patrons still choose to pick up requested material, B-Mail has experienced remarkable growth during its brief existence. Tina Peak oversees the B-Mail operation for PCLC. She reports that, in May 2006, 300 items were mailed to patrons. In August 2008, nearly 5,000 items were mailed. There are seventeen libraries in the cooperative. Within the subset of PCLC libraries that circulate 10,000 or fewer items monthly, B-Mail ranks second or third in circula tion each month. Print books, audiobooks, and movies are available for home delivery, although some libraries in the cooperative do not make their movies eligible for B-Mail.

The B-Mail service operates in a room within the Lake Wales Public Library, where three full-time employees process the requested material. As expected, customer satisfaction among B-Mail users is very high. Peak indicates that there has been little negative feedback about the service, and, as expected, misconceptions about the cost of the service are generally at the heart of any criticism. Citing that there is little overhead involved, Peak explains the cost-per-transaction statistics of the service to those few who do question the viability of the service. The PCLC website features a survey for B-Mail users. For the question "Why do you use B-Mail?" most patrons choose "I prefer to search for my library materials online 24 hours a day, seven days a week."

For all the differences in library size, history, and volume, the stories of home delivery at TSCPL and PCLC have key points in common with MAYL at OCLS. The organizations feel strongly about the value of the service, and they can also point to cost-per-unit studies of the service to illustrate cost-effectiveness. There is also the high satisfaction level of customers, who continually remind the organizations how home delivery helps make the library such a meaningful part of their lives.

Notes

1. Robert T. Jordan, *Tomorrow's Library: Direct Access and Delivery* (New York: R. R. Bowker, 1970).
2. KRC Research, "ALA @ your library Household Survey Results" (2006), www.ala .org/ala/aboutala/offices/ors/reports/krcdetailedslides.pdf.
3. William Sannwald, *Checklist of Library Building Design Considerations*, 5th ed. (Chicago, American Library Association, 2009), 149.

12
Connecting Courier Services

Valerie Horton

Imagine a time when every library patron has access to the contents of every library in the country. For the patron who cannot find the item he wants in his own library's catalog, there is a button on his personal web pages to request it from other sources. This discovery tool provides access to hundreds of millions of volumes held in U.S. libraries. Behind the scenes, the item is requested from the nearest library, and by the next day it is heading toward the requesting patron's library. Delivery takes place within a few days at minimal cost.

This vision is an expansion of the future painted by Steve Coffman in the much-discussed article "Building Earth's Largest Library."[1] Coffman envisions an Amazon.com–like future for libraries. Patrons are no longer locked into a local library catalog but instead go to a global catalog. Coffman suggests that any found library item carry an "available immediately" sticker if it is in the local library, an "available in 24–48 hours" if held by a nearby consortium, and an "available in 2–6 weeks" if the USPS is involved.

Much has been reconsidered since 1999, when Coffman wrote the article, particularly on building the discovery piece of the model. Today many patrons search WorldCat Local first with its forty million plus records, and from WorldCat Local they easily jump to the bibliographic record held at a nearby library. The Firefoxbased "GoGetter!" plug-in is available for download at this writing.[2] On websites with bibliographic sources, GoGetter identifies several sources for finding the desired item, such as a bookstore, an online subscription, or a local library. The discovery piece of the retrieval process has been going through a time of great innovation, thanks largely to the ad hoc Rethinking Resource Sharing group.

The retrieval piece has not been as rigorously challenged to rethinking and new innovations. Even in 1999, Coffman raised the question, "Who's going to pay to deliver all those millions of items to patrons?" Coffman went on to envision a home delivery model like that we discuss in chapter 11. He suggests charging patrons for shipping and delivery as online bookstores do. Unfortunately, an unpublished study done by OCLC in Montana in 2007 found that patrons were not inclined to pay fully for home delivery unless the cost was very low.

So the question remains, other than home delivery, are there other ways of rethinking delivery? In this chapter we explore an alternative method of delivery, namely, linking courier systems to provide inexpensive, rapid delivery between geographically contiguous regions. Existing courier services could deliver to libraries for half the cost of USPS Media Mail, and in a fraction of the time. Although the patron would still have the inconvenience of making a trip to the library to check out the items, there are still many advantages to this model.

The chief characteristic of most library courier services is that they are fast. Most library couriers offer one- to two-day turnaround within their service region. Not only are library couriers services fast, but many are paid for by government funding and there is no direct cost to the participating libraries. Some other library courier services are partially subsidized by state funding or LSTA funds or are provided as part of a package of consortium services to members.

To give an example, in 2007 the largest libraries in the Colorado Library Consortium paid about twenty-five cents to move an item one way. Without the State of Colorado subsidy, the cost per item shipped would roughly double to fifty cents. USPS Media Mail averages $2.30–$2.50, depending on weight and how many zip codes the item passes through.

In chapter 1, a estimate shows that libraries are paying at least $35 million annually to ship ILL materials via the post office. We know library couriers are cheaper and faster than the USPS. Given the justification of poor service and much higher costs, how can we reduce use of the USPS for ILL transactions?

Envision a fleet of trucks passing you on the freeway. On the side of the truck you read "Library Sharing in Action." Through federal legislation, librarians have created a nationwide library delivery system. Fleets of trucks drive long-haul routes across the country. The trucks drop off pallets of bins at one of a dozen regional sorting centers. The bins are transferred to local couriers, who use smaller trucks and vans to deliver to the regional sorting center and finally to the local library. A book moves from New York to Oregon in a matter of days at minimal cost to the library.

This vision is grand, dramatic, expensive, and politically as close to impossible as can be envisioned in these days of budget deficits, recession, and desire for lower taxes. This is not the time to suggest large new programs with high federal tax dollars. Still, there are methods of getting to roughly the same functionality without the huge investments in a federal infrastructure and start-up costs.

LINKING REGIONAL COURIERS SYSTEMS

How do we create the physical delivery piece for the Earth's Largest Library? Assuming the discovery piece is already handled, the next task is to expand local and regional library courier services. At this time, not all parts of the country have access to regional library courier deliveries. We also need to connect to neighboring courier systems, creating a patchwork quilt of linked delivery options. Finally, we must agree on labeling, packaging, and circulation parameters that allow systems to exchange materials easily.

There are a considerable number of library courier services operating in the United States. One recent survey by ALA identified 123 consortium-run courier services.[3] Further, the 2008 delivery study discussed in chapter 2 found twenty-seven states with library courier services. Some states have full coverage (e.g., Michigan and Massachusetts), some states have partial coverage (e.g., Wyoming and Idaho), and a few states have no library couriers services in operation.

We do have successful multistate library courier services to draw from. The Trans-Amigos Express, from Amigos Library Services, delivers to member libraries in Texas, Arkansas, New Mexico, and Oklahoma. Many other regional and statewide services cross state lines. For instance, SWON delivers to libraries in Ohio and Kentucky; the Kansas City Metropolitan Library and Information Network delivers to libraries in Missouri and part of Kansas; and Colorado Library Courier delivers to part of Wyoming. There are academic-only delivery networks that cross state lines, including the Association of Southeastern Research Libraries, which delivers to eighteen university libraries in nine states.

Some courier systems do not deliver to libraries in other states but do link at the borders. One of the best examples is Minnesota's MINITEX Library Information Network and Wisconsin's South Central Library System. These states transfer nearly 100,000 items a year between the two systems, saving well over $500,000 in postage, labor, and mailing materials.

Is there enough library courier service coverage to allow regional linkages? The answer is that it varies around the country. The northern Midwest and most of the eastern seaboard have heavy concentrations of library courier services. It is conceivable that Ohio, Michigan, Minnesota, Illinois, and Wisconsin could connect, but nearby Iowa and Nebraska have only limited delivery to a few universities. A new service launched in May 2009 links libraries in Missouri, Colorado, and part of Kansas. This service, named COKAMO, was already moving a thousand books a week by June 2009 and is expected to save participating libraries over $150,000 in USPS costs the first year and more thereafter. COKAMO is hoping to expand to nearby states in the regions such as Texas, Oklahoma, and others.

For the purposes of this chapter, let's make three assumptions: First, there are currently enough courier services to create a significant number of linked regional service areas around the country. Second, the benefits from regional cooperation would encourage more states and regions to create physical delivery services and link them up. Finally, once low-cost library courier delivery is available, more ILL traffic will shift away from the USPS and move to library courier delivery. Given these assumptions, how would a regional courier linkage function? What standards or shared systems would be required?

CIRCULATION PERIODS, LABELS, AND PACKAGING

Several practical considerations must be addressed before two courier services can link, including consistent labeling, material packaging agreements, circulation parameters, customization of OCLC library records and group creation, regional sorting hubs, and agreed pickup and delivery points.

Some consortia agreed to share the same circulation parameters when they launched direct patron borrowing; others were unable to reach agreement, with dissimilar circulation periods causing confusion and problems for the entire system. A 1996 Library Research Service study found that many libraries at that time shared a three-week loan period.[4] Anecdotally, when the question of circulation periods was raised at a recent national conference, half the audience reported using a three-week loan period; the other half reported using combinations of one, two, three, or four weeks depending on material types and local circumstances.

There is no national standard for circulation loan periods or late fines, nor is there likely to be in the future. To cope with this inconsistency, many consortia, particularly those using the USPS, have built-in grace periods to cover transit time between locations. This lack of agreement will add complexity and difficulty to any agreements between courier systems. Building in a grace period so patrons are not penalized is the best alternative available at this time.

As discussed in chapter 7, systems use several different package labels, from simple codes such as "C123" to OCLC codes to USPS mailing addresses. Regardless of which code is used, it must identify the specific borrowing library. The label may also indicate the lending library. That information is also usually included in a printed-out ILL form that is placed in the library item. The ILL form indicates the patron and usually includes both borrowing and lending library information.

For a regional delivery system to function, another layer of labeling would need to be developed. In a simple two-state system, each participant can easily recognize the other's code, even with quite dissimilar addressing formats in use. But as systems grow and link to more couriers, simple sight recognition of label differences may not work, particularly if multiple sorting centers are used to shift materials between couriers systems.

An alternative would be to use a meta-level code above the local courier code on the print label. An easy meta-level code would be to use the postal codes for the fifty states, such as WI or TX. These postal codes have the advantage of being short and commonly known. Another possibility is to use a shorthand code for the delivery services sorting hub. For instance, the Colorado Library Courier sorts in Denver, so the code could be DEN.

Whereas some couriers use a simple label with limited information, others include substantial amounts of information such as lending library, receiving library, an attention or note to field, date, and others. On such complex labels, there would have to be a way to make the meta-label address stand out for quick recognition and sorting.

The goal with any labeling system is to keep it simple. Since many library courier services are moving millions of items, systems must be designed that keep labor and material costs down. It will be up to the participants involved to decide which meta-labeling to use. Changes will have to be made in whatever system is used to create the labels. Most couriers use a home-grown label creator, which could be difficult to modify. It would be helpful if standard practices were developed to guide implementation of a new label system. It is much easier to start delivery using one system than to change that system later. The more labeling can be standardized across the country, the better for linking courier services.

Current delivery services use a range of packing materials, from the minimal to the excessive with multiple layers of wrappings. Courier services that use overnight carriers have packaging provided by the carrier. Some courier services use padded envelopes and attempt to reuse them. Reusable canvas or nylon bags are also widely used. Many services use a large plastic tote or bin. Inside the tote, library materials are layered loose with a label tucked inside the item or attached with rubber bands to the outside.

It is likely that library materials will be moving in long-haul trucks inside boxes or bins that are stacked on pallets. Large reusable plastic totes appear to be a logical container to stack on pallets. The totes are sturdy enough to be reused thousands of times and have a locking cover to keep out inclement weather. Some system will be required to make sure labels remain secured to the totes as they move between systems.

HOW FEASIBLE IS LINKING COURIERS?

In several states, library courier delivery services cross state lines, usually as part of a consortium that has an established route into the neighboring state. In developing COKAMO, the linked Colorado-Missouri library courier service, Greyhound was found to be the cheapest method of moving items each night from Independence to Denver. In the end, the question is not the ability to link but whether we can afford to link and agree on rules of participation.

From the logistics industry, we know that moving one item is expensive; when you move a box of items, the price for each item drops; but when you move a truckload the price per item can drop to pennies. So the more we move, the less expensive the delivery. This is a real advantage over the USPS, which has the same price for each piece moved. To make cross-state delivery financially feasible for a courier service, volume must be high.

For purposes of illustration, let's assume that two states share 10,000 OCLC ILL transactions a year. The cost of using USPS Media Mail (about $2.40 per paperback, less than 13 ounces) to ship ILL items to the borrowing library and back to the lending library times the number of items moved works out to a cost of roughly $48,000. A quick cost study of paying for a long-haul truck route between Missouri and Colorado suggests that it can be done several days a week for around $15,000–$25,000 a year. Thus the linked library courier would cost half that of USPS service, and transactions could be delivered and sorted each night for a one- or two-day turnaround.

If library courier service is cheaper, ILL personnel are likely to shift their borrowing to states where delivery via courier is possible, and the 10,000 transactions would quickly rise to the 100,000 currently shared by Minnesota and Wisconsin. At first, costs might have to be subsidized until enough volume was generated to keep prices low.

CONCLUSION

In the end, the problem with expanding courier services is not technical, nor with enough volume will it be financial. The issue will be the vision among participating libraries about the importance of resource sharing. The ability to reach agreements on cost sharing, labeling, packaging, shipping arrangements, and acceptable circulation parameters must be made through conversation and compromise. Unfortunately, agreements can be the most difficult thing to achieve, since both parties must agree to maintain the new service over a long time frame.

In 2009, the National Standards Organization (NISO) agreed to start discussions with a group of librarians involved in delivery to see if a standard practices document could be developed. If there could be some agreement on what a library delivery process should look like, the process of reaching the other agreements could be much easier.

Notes

1. Steve Coffman, "Building Earth's Largest Library: Driving into the Future," *Searcher* 7 (March 1999): 34.
2. Rethinking Resource Sharing Initiative, "About GoGetter!" (2008), http://rethinkingresourcesharing.org/getit.html.
3. American Library Association, Association of Specialized and Cooperative Library Agencies, "Library Networks, Cooperatives and Consortia Database" (2008), http://cs.ala.org/ra/lncc/.
4. Library Research Service, "Libraries Nationwide Report Circulation Policies," *Fast Facts* 122 (November 13, 1996): 1–5.

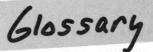

Glossary

Excerpted from the Messenger Courier Association of the Americas. Used with permission, with minor modifications and additions.

Actual Weight: Scale weight of a shipment.

AFV (Alternative Fueled Vehicle): Vehicle powered by a fuel other than gasoline or diesel.

Air Waybill: Contract between shipper and carrier covering international and domestic transportation of cargo to a specified destination. The air waybill may also be referred to as the **source document**.

AVI (Automatic Vehicle Identification): System combining an onboard transponder with roadside receivers to automate identification of vehicles. Uses include electronic toll collection and stolen vehicle detection.

Bill of Lading: Legal document that sets out the details of a shipment such as consigner, consignee, pieces, weight, product description, collect, prepaid, declared value, and any particular service requirements. The bill of lading is signed by the shipper and the driver picking up the freight.

Blanket Wrapping: Specialized transportation handling service designed to protect certain commodities such as furniture, large appliances, household goods, or large office machines such as copiers.

Bulk Shipment: Shipment of loose boxes or pieces.

Cargo Weight: Combined weight of all loads, gear, and supplies on a vehicle.

Cartage Company: Company that provides local (within a town, city, or municipality) pickup and delivery.

CDL (Commercial Driver's License): License that authorizes an individual to operate commercial motor vehicles and buses over 26,000 pounds gross vehicle weight. For operators of freight-hauling trucks, the maximum size that may be driven without a CDL is Class 6 (maximum 26,000 pounds gross vehicle weight).

Chargeable Weight: Charges based on the greater of scale weight or dimensional weight.

COD: Collect upon delivery. Payment is required immediately from the consignee. Not to be confused with **collect**.

Collect: Billing terms in which the consignee, rather than the shipper, receives freight invoices.

Common Carrier: Freight transportation company that serves the general public. May be regular route service (over designated highways on a regular basis) or irregular route (between various points on an unscheduled basis).

Consignee: Party to which a given shipment is addressed on freight bill.

Consolidation: Converting individual smaller shipments into larger, multishipment loads in order to achieve transportation savings.

Container (Shipping Container): Standard-sized rectangular box used to transport freight by ship, rail, and highway. International shipping containers are 20 or 40 feet long, conform to International Standards Organization (ISO) standards, and are designed to fit in ships' holds. Containers are transported on public roads atop a container chassis towed by a tractor. Domestic containers, up to 53 feet long and of lighter construction, are designed for rail and highway use only.

Contract Carrier: Company that transports freight under contract with one or a limited number of shippers.

Cross-Docking: Operational process of transferring freight from one truck to another at a dock facility. Usually involves skidded and shrinkwrapped LTL freight transferred with the use of forklifts.

Cube (Cubic Capacity): Interior volume of a truck body, semitrailer, or trailer, measured in cubic feet.

CWT: Hundredweight increments.

Dangerous Goods: Articles or substances capable of posing a significant risk to health, safety, or property when transported by air. Also referred to as **hazardous materials** or **restricted articles**. The following are dangerous goods that must be declared at time of booking: oil-based paint and thinners (flammable liquids); industrial solvents; insecticides; garden chemicals (fertilizers, poisons); lithium batteries (not in cameras); magnetized materials; machinery (chain saws or outboard engines containing fuel); fuel for camp stoves, lanterns, torches, or heating elements; automobile batteries; infectious substances; any compound, liquid, or gas that has toxic characteristics; bleach; flammable adhesives; perfume; alcohol.

Dead-Heading: Operating a truck without cargo.

Declared Value: Value of goods declared by the shipper for the purposes of determining charges and/or establishing the limit of the carrier's liability for loss, damage, or delay. Valuation charges are assessed to shippers who declare a value of goods higher than the value of the carrier's limits of liability.

Dedicated Trucks: Trucks that contain freight from a single exclusive shipper.

Desktop Delivery: Inside delivery of small shipment directly to end user's desk.

DIM (Dimensional Weight): Space or volume of a shipment. Determined by multiplying the length by the width by the height and dividing the product by 194 for domestic shipments or by 166 for international shipments.

For-Hire Carrier: Company in the business of transporting freight belonging to others.

Gateway: Last city within a country from which a shipment departs when going to an international destination. For example, a shipment that travels from Denver, Colorado, to Chicago, Illinois, to Paris, France, would list Chicago, Illinois, as the gateway.

Hazmat (Hazardous Materials): Classification of dangerous materials from the U.S. Environmental Protection Agency. Transport of hazardous materials is strictly regulated by the U.S. Department of Transportation.

Hours-of-Service: U.S. Department of Transportation safety regulations that govern the hours of service of commercial vehicle drivers engaged in interstate trucking operations.

IAC (Indirect Air Carrier): Any person or entity within the United States not in possession of a Federal Aviation Administration air carrier operating certificate who undertakes to engage indirectly in air transportation of property and uses for all or any part of such transportation the services of a passenger air carrier. Each indirect air carrier must adopt and carry out a security program that meets TSA requirements.

JIT (Just-in-Time): Manufacturing system that depends on frequent, small deliveries of parts and supplies to keep on-site inventory to a minimum.

Known Shipper: Person or entity authorized to ship cargo on passenger air carriers. A systematic approach is used to assess risk and determine the legitimacy of shippers. Passenger air carriers and indirect air carriers must comply with a broad range of specific security requirements to qualify their clients as known shippers.

Lessee: Company or individual that leases and uses vehicles.

Lessor: Company that leases vehicles to others.

Logbook: Book carried by truck drivers in which they record their hours of service and duty status for each 24-hour period. Required in interstate commercial trucking by the U.S. Department of Transportation.

Loose Shipment: Shipment that is tendered as individual boxes or pieces. Also referred to as a **bulk shipment.**

LTL (Less-Than-Truckload): Quantity of freight less than that required for the application of a truckload (TL) rate; usually less than 10,000 pounds.

LTL Carrier: Trucking company that consolidates LTL cargo for multiple destinations on one vehicle.

Mixed Charges: Shipping and other charges split between the shipper and the receiver (consignee).

OS&D (Over, Short and Damaged): Report designed to provide all exceptions from a consolidated shipment once received by delivering carrier. This report is critical in the transfer of cargo liability.

Oversized Package: Package between 84 inches and 130 inches in length and girth but less than 30 pounds. Such a package is rated at the 30-pound small package rate (standard UPS provision).

Owner-Operator: People who own and operate their own truck(s).

P&D: Pickup and delivery.

Payload: Weight of the cargo being hauled.

Pedal Runs: LTL shipments loaded onto trailer such that the truck can drop them off in order on a given route.

Pick & Pack: Fulfillment of orders of more than one SKU into a shipping container from the warehouse floor.

POD: Proof of delivery.

Prepaid: Shipper responsible for payment of charges.

Private Carrier: Business that operates trucks primarily for the purpose of transporting its own products and raw materials. The principal business activity of a private carrier is not transportation.

Pup Trailer: Short semitrailer, usually 26–32 feet long, with a single axle.

Recovery: Act of picking up a shipment at the destination.

Recovery Time: Amount of time it takes to process a shipment and have it available for pickup after a flight arrives at the final destination.

Scale Weight: Actual weight of a shipment.

Shipping Weight: "Dry" weight of a truck including all standard equipment but excluding fuel and coolant.

Sliding Fifth Wheel: Fifth wheel mounted to a mechanism that allows it to be moved back and forth for the purpose of adjusting the distribution of weight on the tractor's axles. Also provides the capability to vary vehicle combination lengths.

Sortation: Sorting items at a warehouse for delivery the next day or onboard sorting by drivers.

Tender: Act of dropping off a shipment at the origin.

Third Party: Person/company paying shipping and related charges is neither the shipper nor the consignee.

TL (Truckload): Quantity of freight required to fill a trailer; usually more than 10,000 pounds.

TL Carrier: Trucking company that dedicates trailers to a single shipper's cargo, as opposed to an LTL carrier, which transports the consolidated cargo of several shippers and makes multiple deliveries.

Trip Leasing: Leasing a company's vehicle to another transportation provider for a single trip.

Unknown Shipper: Person or entity who does not meet the security status of a known shipper. Unknown shippers cannot ship cargo on passenger air carriers.

Warehousing In Fee: Charge associated with receiving freight into a warehouse. This fee covers the costs of labor, forklift handling, and storage of the freight. Typically, the in fee is charged on a per-pallet basis.

Warehousing Out Fee: Charge associated with moving freight out of a warehouse. This fee covers the costs of labor, forklift handling, and retrieving the freight from inventory. Typically, the out fee is charged on a per-pallet basis.

White Glove Delivery: In-home delivery and light assembly of related items as well as removal of all packaging materials.

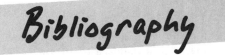

Bibliography

Prepared and annotated by Robin Dean

Bessant, R. 1997. *Delivery of Library Materials in Wisconsin.* Prepared for Division for Libraries and Community Learning, Bureau for Interlibrary Loan and Resource Sharing. Madison, WI: Department of Public Instruction.

Bessant, a consultant for the Wisconsin Division for Libraries and Community Learning, describes her process of determining the cost-effectiveness of connecting Wisconsin's regional courier services to a statewide delivery network. Her article includes a comparison of weekly three-day and five-day delivery, a summary of the proposals received from different courier services, a review of the courier services offered by other states at the time, and the different network and cost-sharing models that might be considered when expanding service. She found that Northern Waters was currently better served by conducting ILL through the USPS with the rest of the state.

Burkholder, S. A. 1992. "By Our Own Bootstraps: Making Document Delivery Work in Oregon." *Computers in Libraries* 12 (11): 19–24 (special section: Document Delivery).

This article traces the development of a statewide courier system in Oregon, which grew out of the informal findings of a subcommittee and was largely a grassroots push by librarians in the state. Since this project was not supported by state or federal funds, money was a major concern. Burkholder discusses the steps taken to make the service self-sufficient, affordable, and efficient. Creative cost-splitting and integration with local courier services already in place contributed to the project's success. The summary offers a thoughtful examination of the benefits and drawbacks of creating such a simple, noncentralized, hands-off system.

Fiels, K. M., and R. P. Naylor. 1990. *Delivery of Information and Materials between Libraries: The State of the Art.* Proceedings of the June 1990 ASCLA

Multi-LINCS Preconference. Association of Specialized and Cooperative Library Agencies. Chicago: American Library Association.

This compilation includes several speeches and presentations that focus on the development of physical delivery in Illinois, New Jersey, Washington, and Oregon. Each presentation explains how the states analyzed the needs of their geographic areas and how they selected delivery services that would fit those needs at a reasonable cost and maximum efficiency.

Gassler, R. S. 1985. "Pricing for Efficiency, Equity, and Simplicity: A Model Policy for an Interlibrary Courier Service." *Journal of Library Administration* 6 (2): 83–100.

Gassler, an economist, consulted for a midwest interlibrary service to recommend an efficient, equitable, and simple courier pricing structure for libraries should state funds for ILL delivery fail. Self-sufficiency is not a requirement; Gassler assumes that there will always be some sort of outside funding to help run a courier system. He favors assigning an equal portion of the fixed costs (administrative, wages, vehicles) and traveling costs (fuel, maintenance) to all libraries.

Geiser, C., and R. Miller. 1996. "GMRLC Negotiations for an Interstate Courier: History, Results and Trends." *Journal of Library Administration* 23 (1/2): 5–22.

This article describes the Greater Midwest Regional Library Cooperation's experience in creating an interstate delivery system. The authors describe the RFP process and how they chose FedEx as their method of delivery. The whole idea of interstate ILL was new to most of the vendors, institutions, and even librarians involved in the project. The authors discuss some of the unexpected stumbling blocks, such as the impossibility of all the states signing a blanket contract with FedEx.

Graham, A. 2000. "Resource Sharing within the Western North Carolina Library Network: Faculty and Student Perspective." *Journal of Library Administration* 31 (1): 41–54.

Graham discusses user awareness of and satisfaction with the physical document delivery system of a small network of academic libraries. Lack of satisfaction is related to a less than 100 percent fill rate and slower delivery speeds. Dissatisfied users "did not feel that resource sharing was an adequate substitute for owning the materials, primarily because of the time lost in obtaining the material, inconvenience, and the lost ability to discover good resources through browsing" (48). Graham proposes ways to increase user satisfaction and improve document delivery.

Hamilton, P. 2004. "Visions of Statewide Document Delivery." *OLA Quarterly* 9/10 (4/1): 8–9.

This short article describes the Oregon library system's realization that a proposed statewide library catalog would increase demand for an efficient statewide library materials delivery service. Short- and long-term goals for preparing the courier system for the demands of a statewide catalog are listed. This article may be useful for courier systems looking to set goals.

Helmer, John F. 1999. "Orbis Courier Service: The Resurrection of a Collaborative Success." *OLA Quarterly* 5 (1): 8–10.

This article follows up the Burkholder 1992 article (see above); the lack of administrative or centralized control in the Oregon/Washington courier service led to a crisis. The crux of the problem was vague contract terms and fluctuating rates, exacerbated by the fact that people concerned about the courier had no way to communicate with each other. A central administrator was chosen, lines of communication were opened, and a fixed, affordable yearly contract was negotiated.

Julian, G. 1996. "Truck and High-Tech: Document Delivery in the '90s." *Serials Librarian* 28 (3/4): 275–81.

This article summarizes a workshop on physical versus electronic document delivery. It cites speed of service as the most important factor in the success of any method of document delivery. It includes a cost analysis of shipping original physical materials as opposed to scanning/photocopying articles and sending the reproductions. Using a regional courier service to send original physical materials, placing the burden of reproduction (if necessary) on the user, was found to be more cost efficient. The emphasis of the workshop is that electronic transmission (which has the benefit of speed) is a complement to, not a replacement for, physical delivery (which was then cheaper and less labor intensive than electronic methods). Almost twenty years later, it would be interesting to know if electronic document delivery is still notably more expensive and less labor intensive than physical delivery.

Library Research Service. 2003. "Courier Service by Regional Systems Saves Libraries Millions of Dollars Annually over Alternative Delivery Methods." *Fast Facts: Recent Statistics from the Library Research Service.* ED3/110.10/ No. 191 (March 16). www.lrs.org/documents/fastfacts/191_courier.pdf.

The Colorado statewide courier system was found to be vastly less expensive than shipping materials with the USPS, UPS, or FedEx. Twenty-five public, five academic, four special, and one school library participated in the survey, a mixture of small, medium, and large districts/institutions. This sample seems to be intended as a representative, not comprehensive, survey of Colorado libraries.

Lietzau, Z. 2007. "Statewide Courier Saves Libraries Thousands in Shipping Costs Each Year." *Fast Facts: Recent Statistics from the Library Research Service.* ED3/110.10/No. 251. www.lrs.org/documents/fastfacts/251_courier.pdf.

This *Fast Facts* is a reprise of the 2003 LRS study; it surveys a similar number and type of libraries and compares the cost of courier usage to the cost of USPS, UPS, or FedEx delivery. The courier system is still greatly more cost-effective, not only because of its rates per item but because it is easier to package and prepare materials for the courier than for any commercial shipping service. The study estimates that the cheapest alternative to the courier, the USPS, would be 3.5 times more expensive than the courier.

Massie, D. 2000. "The International Sharing of Returnable Library Materials." *Interlending and Document Supply* 28 (3): 110–15.

This article cites two main barriers to international lending: cost and fear/confusion about the lending process and the accountability of foreign institutions for the materials received. Most of the article is a report on the activities of the SHARES International ILL Task Force, part of RLG. Massie discusses some of the task force successes in easing international loan for its members and its goals going forward, such as reducing shipping costs, revising current policies to reflect a more global membership, and creating a best practices document for shipping to different countries. Some of the survey data collected by SHARES about its member institutions will be useful to people curious about the status of international ILL.

Pierson, S. K. 2007. "Montana Library Courier System: Is There Potential?" University of Southern Mississippi SLIS Master's Project. www.clicweb.org/movingmountains/Pierson_S_FinalPROJECT080107.pdf.

The Montana State Library, as part of a study on the feasibility and advisability of a statewide courier system, conducted surveys of other states' courier activities and regional Montana courier activities. Pierson's thesis includes a literature review, extensive bibliography, and appendixes with the survey questions and aggregated answers. Her analysis of the survey results shows that reliability is the most important aspect of a courier service to libraries, followed distantly by cost and turnaround time, and that courier services generally save money and time over other methods of physical delivery.

Ruhnke, C. 2005. "The Meaning of Delivery in Illinois." *Illinois Libraries* 86 (1): 37–38.

This short article has a few facts on the volume of materials Illinois libraries move on their courier and some hypotheses about how and why so many items are moved. The information is not substantial, but a few of the citations may be of further interest.

Shrauger, K. J. 2002. "Courier Services Come to Arkansas." *Arkansas Libraries* 59 (6): 4–8.

This article offers concise and detailed information on the structure and some of the policies (packing, pricing, etc.) of the Arkansas library courier system. Advantages of the courier system include less packaging time, no weight restrictions, and the ability to move non-ILL items (correspondence, giveaways). It also greatly improved turnaround and delivery time to patrons when used as a fulfillment method through OCLC. In nine months, half the libraries on the courier recovered the yearly courier fee in mailing cost savings. Shrauger anticipates that the system will become more, not less, cost-effective as it expands.

Contributors

Lori Ayre began working with libraries in 2000 after a fifteen-year career managing technology, leading projects, and designing information systems. Ayre's consulting firm, the Galecia Group, has done a wide variety of work for libraries and consortia including technology consulting, systems analysis, software specifications development, and management consulting. She is currently focused on resource sharing, delivery, materials handling, and open-source applications.

Brenda Bailey-Hainer has since 2006 been president and CEO of BCR, a nonprofit membership organization that serves libraries primarily in an eleven-state region in the West. Previously she was director of networking and resource sharing at the Colorado State Library, where she created and managed statewide projects related to resource sharing, digitization, and virtual reference. Her past experience includes various positions at OCLC, CARL Corporation, and UnCover document delivery service as well as several academic libraries. At the Colorado State Library she served as interim manager of the Colorado Library Courier and served on the state's courier committee. She was a co-organizer of the 2005 Moving Mountains Symposium held in Denver.

Robin Dean works in the records management and digital initiatives programs at the University of Denver. Though she spends most of her time in the digital world, Robin's work at the Colorado Library Consortium taught her a healthy respect for the coordination it takes to get things to people. She received her MLIS from the University of Denver in 2008.

Ivan Gaetz is dean of libraries at Regis University, Denver. He earned his MLS in 1988 from the University of Alberta and has worked in government, theological, public, and academic libraries in Alberta, British Columbia, New York, and Colorado. His library work has focused on promoting and advancing library collaboration, and he regards document delivery systems as key to interlibrary partnerships. A member of the Colorado Alliance of Research Libraries, he organized and chairs the Shared Collection Development Committee and is chair of the Colorado Academic Library Consortium (2008/9).

David Millikin earned BS and BA from Ohio State in 2000 with a double-major in transportation and logistics and operations management. He has worked in various positions at Greif, Inc., a global industrial packaging manufacturer, in its sourcing and supply chain department. In 2006 he became a certified purchasing manager. He was a product manager of library logistics at OCLC and has developed new home delivery and storage management solutions for libraries.

Jim Myers is currently head of circulation for the Orange County Library System (OCLS) in Orlando, Florida. Prior to taking charge of circulation, Jim managed the OCLS home delivery service, MAYL, for seven years. From 2004 to 2006, Jim was also the project manager for Healthy Connections, a two-year, multimedia health initiative sponsored in part by the National Library of Medicine, which won the 2006 state-level award from the National Commission on Libraries and Information Science.

Lisa Priebe joined the Colorado Library Consortium (CLiC) in 2005 as a regional consultant and has been assistant director since 2007. She was the project manager for the development of the courier management system that streamlined courier functions for participating institutions and CLiC staff. In addition to working with the courier, Lisa is responsible for managing cooperative purchases and vendor awards along with handling some of CLiC's internal operations.

Greg Pronevitz has been regional administrator of the Northeast Massachusetts Regional Library System (NMRLS) since 1998. NMRLS, one of six regional library systems in Massachusetts, serves three hundred member libraries in fifty-four communities, providing training, consulting, electronic content, and physical delivery of library materials. Prior to his appointment at NMRLS, Greg was an assistant director at OHIONET and held technical services positions at the Ohio State University, Chemical Abstracts Service, and the Center for Research Libraries.

Melissa Stockton earned her MA in library science from Texas Woman's University in 1989. Since that time she has worked in several multitype consortia, an academic library, and the library vendor arena. At the Colorado Alliance, Melissa managed several library systems for a group of academic and public libraries.

At Regis University; she started the Library Systems Department and also managed access services, including the ILL department. Melissa started Quipu Group in 2005 with two partners to provide programming and development services to libraries. In 2007, Quipu Group released Library2Library, a courier management system developed in partnership with the Colorado Library Consortium.

Index